CU00650209

This book is an incredible gift and comes at an
ever knew Lonnie Frisbee will immediately be   , ...ou as 1 was to
"hear" Lonnie's own voice. Those who never knew or heard Lonnie will "get
it"—the power, authenticity, simplicity, passion, and humor of a simple,
broken man who lived to hear and obey God's voice. This book is essential to
understanding what we know as the Jesus movement.

—Pastor Kenn Gulliksen
Founder of Vineyard Christian Fellowship

Every movement of the Holy Spirit has its strengths and weaknesses. Why?
God uses man. The Jesus People movement changed my life forever. I tasted,
experienced, and absorbed an entirely new and different culture to
Christianity. Lonnie Frisbee was a forerunner and trailblazer of this amazing
movement where Jesus Christ was kept central. I am so grateful for Lonnie's
sacrifice and the wake he helped create with signs and wonders following.
Blessings to all who read this series of books and become trailblazers as well.

—Dr. James W. Goll
Founder of God Encounters Ministries and International Best-Selling Author

Roger Sachs brings Lonnie back to us. Even if it's just for a little while, we get
to feel as though we are right there for the times when the Holy Spirit was
poured out upon us, when miracles happened in front of our eyes, and when
an unlikely vessel for God's mercy named Lonnie ministered the love of God
to us from deep in his heart. One of the great privileges of my life was to
minister alongside Lonnie Frisbee. Thank you, Roger, for reminding us to
look for the miracles around us every day.

—Debby Kerner Rettino, DMin
Author and Singer-Songwriter

Roger has captured the heart and life of Lonnie Frisbee! We are in the
beginning of another wave, and I believe that it is very prophetic and timely
that we get to discover the raw and vulnerable revivalist who changed nations
with the simple gospel of Jesus!

—Chad Dedmon
Pastor at Bethel Church, Redding

Lonnie was my younger brother, but when he started walking in his calling, he became like my spiritual father. He's the one who made it possible for me to come to the Lord. My brother said he was a modern mystic. He was certainly an evangelist, catalyst, and forerunner. It wasn't something he decided to be—it was deep within him. The Holy Spirit worked through Lonnie, and even when it was a simple thing, it was a God thing. I believe the Lord chose my brother because, for one, God uses the weak, broken, and foolish things of the world to confound the wise and so-called mighty. But I also think it was Lonnie's childlike faith, open and vulnerable lifestyle, and his trust in God that qualified him—that made him willing to say *yes* to the incredible call on his life.

—Stan Frisbee

Lonnie Frisbee is a forgotten wild heart who ignited a generation to fall more in love with Jesus. I grew up in the Anaheim Vineyard where Lonnie was catalytic to release the Holy Spirit in a profound way. The foundations that have been laid in my life have been influenced by his willingness to become a vessel of the Holy Spirit. Lonnie's story encourages me because it proves that God can take anyone with a yielded heart, regardless of their past or imperfections, and impact a generation.

Lonnie was a person of his time, born for his generation. He was like a Moses leading people out of bondage and into freedom. It's now time for a new *Jesus Revolution* to arise, for a Joshua generation to go beyond what he accessed and to enter into the Promised Land of our era. Lonnie paved the way. Let's ride on the momentum set before us, dive into family, and cling to Jesus with everything inside. Hang on tight; I have a feeling the wildest ride of our lives is waiting for us just around the corner.

—Jennifer A. Miskov, PhD
Author of Ignite Azusa: Positioning for a New Jesus Revolution, *Speaker, and Founding Director of Destiny House*

Not by Might, Nor by Power

The Jesus Revolution
SECOND EDITION

Also in this series:

Not by Might, Nor by Power

Jesusfolket är här

The Jesus Revolution
SECOND EDITION

Lonnie Frisbee
with Roger Sachs

NOT BY MIGHT, NOR BY POWER: THE JESUS REVOLUTION
Lonnie Frisbee with Roger Sachs
Second edition © 2017 by Freedom Publications

First edition © 2012 by Freedom Publications
All rights reserved.

This book is authorized under contract with Lonnie Frisbee. The views and opinions expressed are those of Lonnie Frisbee. Some names have been changed to protect the privacy of individuals.

Freedom Crusade
P.O. Box 2583
Santa Maria, CA 93457

www.freedomcrusade.org
www.lonnierayfrisbee.com
info@lonnierayfrisbee.com

Cover photo courtesy of Jack Cheetham. Used by permission.

ISBN 0-9785433-3-5

Printed in the United States

Dedicated to Kathryn Kuhlman

TABLE OF CONTENTS

Foreword

I've written and rewritten this foreword several times, not because it was difficult to put together, but because each time I finished, there was so much more to say about Lonnie!

In writing, they say that great adjectives make for great material. In Lonnie's case, I run out of adjectives pretty quickly. It seems like there are not enough words in the English language to accurately describe this very unique individual. However, here's a few: brilliant, controversial, gifted off the scale, humble, proud, bold, transparent, teachable, prophetic, friendly, standoffish, childish, worldly, passionate, healed, broken. The list goes on, but in most cases, whatever adjective you could choose, he was probably equally the polar opposite as well.

One major lesson I've learned in life is this: If you want to be used by God, it will require risk. You cannot and must not worry too much about what others think about you. Those who accomplish a lot, risk a lot.

A very important mentor of mine gave me some vital counsel when I first entered into the pastoral ministry. I was seeking to hear the voice of the Spirit, pray for the sick, etc. He wisely told me, "If you want to learn how to pray in power and effectiveness, then hang out with someone who is doing that well." The one person in my circle who was being used by God the most was obvious to me. That was Lonnie Frisbee. My only question was whether or not he would be available for someone like me to tag along and ask questions.

Thank God for a series of weekly meetings in Long Beach, California. Lonnie held Monday night meetings dedicated to teaching and practicing the gifts of the Spirit. Much of what I carry in my heart and what has made me effective over the past couple of decades in planting churches has come from those Monday night meetings held at a Long Beach church.

Even though at the time I had to get up early the next day for my teaching job at a school in the San Fernando Valley, an hour and a half away, it was well worth losing sleep to hang out really late with Lonnie at a Denny's diner after the meetings.

Those Monday evening gatherings were amazing. The move of the Spirit was dramatic. What I'd only read about in church history was going on in those meetings. Healings were happening each week. Gifts were imparted, sometimes even to those who were downright scoffing, just as it was with a group of teenage boys who were sitting on the back row one night. Lonnie asked them to come forward. They came down laughing at him, but as they stood there momentarily, God's Spirit clearly touched them. They began to shake. He asked if they had ever prayed in the Spirit. They tried to say no, but it was difficult to get their words out.

Lonnie then loudly said, "Okay, now speak in tongues!"

Immediately the entire group of boys began to speak in a prayer language. My theology was being totally messed with! I thought it was necessary for a *sincere* person to seek God, to be open to the gifts, blah, blah, blah. Here was God moving differently than my assumptions.

Lonnie is perhaps the only preacher in history who had his own theme song. When musicians were nearby and available, he had it played. The words were simple, but they reflected the heart of a guy who couldn't get enough of two things: more of God and more friends.

Friend, will you remember me,
Think of me,
Pray for me?
And when another day is through,
I'll still remember you.

Steve Sjogren
Author and Kindness Coach
May 2012

Preface to the Second Edition

As you read Lonnie's story, you will notice that he jumps around in time occasionally. Well, this is 2017, and we are rereleasing this first book in the *Not By Might, Nor By Power* series, which was published in 2012. At that time we were on a very tight budget, didn't have a professional editor, and many other constraints. However, without any promotion except a few Facebook postings and word of mouth, the book reached a lot of people with very encouraging feedback. I received emails and letters from people across the United States, as well as England, Europe, New Zealand, and other countries. I even got a long email from a young man in Chile who shared how Lonnie's story powerfully changed his life. That is exactly what Lonnie wanted his story to do, and I know he is looking down on us, saying, "High five!" (When I got up this morning to write this preface, our digital clock displayed 5:55—very cool!)

One of the emails I received was from a young gal named Jennifer Westbrook, who had never even heard of Lonnie Frisbee. She had been touched by the book, saw that I was working on another volume, and volunteered to be "another set of eyes." She is a professional editor with much training and experience. To make a long story short, she has moved from Redding, CA, to Santa Maria and has now been with us for well over a year. She helped immensely in the recently released *Not by Might, Nor by Power: The Great Commission*, Book Two. Believe me, Jennifer has been an invaluable addition to our little team, which includes Jason Francia, Debbie LaMunyon, my daughter Jenna, who designed the last two covers among a thousand other tasks, my son John, who also edits and is just finishing up his master's degree in English, and my wife, Roxanne. So now that I have all this talented help in my old age (I will be seventy in September), I need to stop saying, "We will fake it 'til we make it."

By the way, Lonnie would be turning sixty-eight years old this June. What would Lonnie Frisbee have been like in his sixties and seventies? I've thought about that many times. I'm sure it would have been a whole bunch more of the same—and then some. But the story doesn't end here on earth, which is a radical truth and the hope we all have in Jesus. We will soon enough see our Lord face-to-face and be reunited with Lonnie as well!

Anyway, in rereleasing the first book, *Not by Might, Nor by Power: The Jesus Revolution*, we have a new cover, additions from friends and coworkers of Lonnie, endorsements, and so on. We corrected some typos and formatting problems, and basically improved the flow of Lonnie's story without losing his voice. It has been a labor of love, and I thank all who have contributed, including Charlie Wear, who has been a blessing from the beginning. I also want to thank all of you who have read both of the *Not By Might* books so far—and please continue to pray for the final volume, subtitled *Set Free*, to be completed in a timely way, hopefully within a year or so!

Many Blessings,

Roger Sachs

Introduction

Many, many people are interested in the supernatural. Hollywood movies are filled with supernatural themes, superheroes, villains, and cosmic battles between good and evil. This is a real-life, true story about a person who hundreds, if not thousands, of people around the world claim had supernatural abilities. He is not with us anymore. He died in 1993 in the midst of controversy and disgrace. However, during the last three years of his life, he was compelled to tell his own story.

Others have written about him in books. He was in *Look*, *Time*, and other magazines. There is a documentary about his life and death that is available for anyone to see. You can look him up online and read opinions by both friend and foe. His name is Lonnie Frisbee, and this is Lonnie's story in his own words, from his own perspective, as he lived it out.

I had the privilege of being a close friend. Lonnie asked me to help tell his story. I was more than willing and honored. I am not a professional writer, but together we audiotaped, filmed, and documented his life for most of those last three years. I am also among the eyewitnesses who saw the supernatural powerfully at work in this unique person, who left us so soon. But what an impact he made in his short forty-three years.

Some of his accounts will sound like a Hollywood script from some gifted writer with a huge imagination, but that is not the case. This is the truth, with documented evidence that is overwhelming. Lonnie believed that his story would be used by God as a roadmap to recovery—a roadmap to life—for a multitude. That was his motivation, as well as an honest desire to set the story straight.

Lonnie never imagined that it would take almost twenty years after his death to get his story out there. However, after he died on March 12, 1993, somehow I knew that everything was to be put "on hold" for a season. It was not time for Lonnie to tell his own story.

I now see the wisdom in the long delay. This is the right time, and I am very excited about what will happen next. Not many people can speak from the grave in such a powerful way as Lonnie does in the following "first-person" account—because it's "not by might, nor by power, but by the Spirit of God!"

Check out his story with an open mind and open heart. There is much to be gleaned from the life and times of Lonnie Frisbee.

God bless you!

Roger Sachs

"Any story sounds true until someone tells the other side and sets the record straight."

Proverbs 18:17 TLB

"Not by might, nor by power, but by my spirit, saith the LORD of hosts."

Zechariah 4:6

ONE

Listen to My Servant

I LOOK DOWN the beach. It is one of those beautiful Northern California coastlines with lots of driftwood, fog, and powerful waves crashing on the rocks with thunderous slaps. It is 1970, the middle of winter. The fog coming in is cold, but I feel nothing but exhilaration as I continue my long walk alone in this rugged beauty. I can see down the coast probably about a mile. Taking my time, I walk and walk, and then—*far out*, I see the opening of a really large cave. Inside, I'm amazed at the ceiling structure. It goes way up and is like being inside a subterranean room. This is definitely beautiful and cool. I've never seen a cave this big on a Northern California beach.

I say to myself, being a good "glossolalia"-practicing hippy, "The echo to worship God in here is perfect!" I start singing. As I worship the Lord, a presence fills the cave. It is holy. It is ethereal. I hear the Lord say in my mind, "There are five people coming down the beach right now. I want you to tell them about me." The sweetness of his voice fills the air. I was worshipping in the spirit, lifting my hands, and then God met me in worship—with divine guidance.

Now, keep in mind, I had just walked all over this beach, and there was no one around but the seagulls. It was totally deserted. Like I said, it's the middle of winter, and even with my jacket on, it is miserably, Northern California cold! However, as I walk outside of the cave, there are five guys coming down the beach toward me like magic, **just like he told me in the Spirit!**

I walk up to the five young men, with all the confidence of someone who has *just heard from God*, and say, "Excuse me, but I'm a minister. Will you please give me a few minutes of your time so that I can explain some things? Things that I feel I MUST tell you! I believe the Lord has spoken to me, telling me to share Christ with you, so please listen."

I stoop down and begin to draw the four spiritual laws in the sand. "Did you know that God loves you and has a wonderful plan for your life?" (That is law number one!) I had practically memorized the entire "Four Spiritual Laws" tract along with its supporting scriptures.[1] It was developed and put out there by Bill Bright from Campus Crusade for Christ back in the sixties. The other three laws basically reveal that we are separated from God by our sins and failures, that Jesus is the only answer and provision, and finally, that we must each personally receive Jesus Christ as Savior and Lord in order to know and eternally experience God's love and plan for our lives.

So I sketched diagrams of Christ being invited into one's life. Four of the young men listened intently to everything, but the fifth didn't. As I continued to draw circles in the sand, this fifth man, Roger (not Roger Sachs), violently and with all kinds of anger said, "I don't believe in God!" When I tried to talk, he argued and injected mockery, but I had no argument for him.

Scripture says that we should avoid arguments and quarrels.[2] So instead of arguing, I kept leading the conversation right back to witnessing for Christ and being kind and patient. Nevertheless, Roger became even louder and more obnoxious. He began to throw things. As the volume increased, he seemed to be on the verge of explosion. I know where that kind of combustion comes from. I've seen plenty of violence and signs of violence. I was also tuned in to spiritual warfare. So I said real loud, "**Be quiet!**"—and then he was. The Spirit of God gave me power in Jesus' name to quiet whatever was rising up in this guy.

I continued to tell them about Christ, how we must dethrone our egos and surrender to his loving will for our lives. I kept witnessing for the Lord with all my heart. I threw in a little of my own testimony here and there, which kept me busy for about an hour. At the end of the Four Spiritual Laws tract is a question: "Is there any good reason why you wouldn't want to accept Christ *right now*?"

Four of my new friends said, "Yes, we would like to accept Christ. Thank you, Lonnie, for sharing your heart with us." The four men prayed and made a decision to accept Jesus into their hearts as their personal Savior!

Then, of course, I had to baptize them because I was never going to see them again. We stripped down to our underwear on the freezing beach, and I baptized all four of them in that cold winter surf. I was elated, and believe me, I was *warm* even though the water was stinging cold. **He** kept me warm, just as if I were wearing a wetsuit. The waves were quite large, so all I had to do was hold their noses, and as the waves came crashing over the candidates for baptism, the Lord cleverly immersed them. I didn't. I would only line each of them up quickly as a new swell formed, and then the wave would crash over them and baptize them. It was such a special time. Finally, we said goodbye and embraced.

I turned to Roger and said, "Goodbye. I'm sorry that it didn't work out for you like it did with your friends. But I'm absolutely delighted that your buddies got saved."

As we parted, a group of my friends came down the beach looking for me. I was way overdue. I always seem to keep people waiting when the Holy Spirit uses me. I just forget about everything else that is going on.

A little later while back with my friends on the beach, this young man, Roger, suddenly came running up to us. He had a very powerful "struck" look on his face. It's the only way I can describe his expression. I'll never forget it. He said, "As I was walking down the beach out toward the water, a voice came out of heaven and said to me: "**Listen to my servant!**"

Roger was positively shaken to his core that God had actually spoken to him. He cried out, "I didn't listen to anything you said at all," as tears streamed down his face. "I didn't listen to anything. I didn't hear one word. You must tell me *EVERYTHING* that you said before!" He was pleading and begging me to tell him everything again. Roger was completely broken. A short time before, he was coming out with existentialism and all kinds of heady stuff in his arguments. He said he was a communist atheist. (*How interesting! I never met a communist before!*) Not only was he in rebellion against authority, he was in rebellion against his parents and God. He was an intelligent young man who had just had his mind blown by a voice from the sky.

In our previous encounter I had let him go because he was fighting the witness of Christ so hard. I shut him down with the authority given to us as believers. I ignored him, kept my focus on the other four, and brought them in. The whole thing was totally radical! Not only was the sweetness of the Holy Spirit in the cave, but God also told me specific information that ended up being exactly true. When I came out of the cave, there were five guys walking up the beach toward me. Incredible! I was able to take four and lead them to Christ. Then God spoke to Roger in an audible voice from the atmosphere, and along with my company of friends who were all believers, we graciously shared Jesus with Roger.

It was a perfect New Testament scene. There were men and women there, and we had a fire going. (You can build fires on most Northern California beaches.) We all sat around the fire, and I began to explain to Roger how God had a plan for him if he would only yield to the lordship of Jesus Christ and the kingdom of God. He prayed! By the way, I stripped down again to my wet underwear and baptized him in the ocean. Then the Lord baptized him with the Holy Spirit. So he got saved, baptized with water, and baptized in the Holy Spirit, all at the same time. HE WAS CONVERTED!!

Then Roger said, "You can't leave me here!" He didn't know who we were or where we were from.

I said, "I'm going to challenge you."

"In what way?" he asked.

"I feel that this is such a unique setting here by the water and the open beach, with people being converted and the blessing of the Lord so strongly on this time. I feel that the Lord would say to you, 'Follow me!'"

It was such a powerful moment! I said to our former atheist, "We absolutely love you, Roger, and are one hundred percent for your success in Christianity. It's very powerful the way that God chose to bring you in. Not many people have heard God's audible voice." (I had never heard an audible voice up to that time.) I challenged him: "You drop your net and follow the Lord. Come with me. If you come back to Southern California with me, the Lord will change your life even more."

Roger went home and told his parents that he had become a Christian. He drew all his money out of the bank, quickly sold his motorcycle, and dropped everything that he knew in this world, all because he heard a supernatural voice say, "Listen to my servant."

We flew down on Air California and drove to Calvary Chapel Costa Mesa, which was in the midst of the sizzling Jesus People Revival. There were literally thousands of people assembling around the ministry of Calvary Chapel. It was during a veritable crescendo of the Holy Spirit bringing people to Jesus.

That Wednesday night when we pulled in, it was my night to speak. I did the regular Wednesday night service for years. Roger didn't realize that I actually was a church minister. Because of my radical appearance with the long hair and beard, perhaps he thought I was a Christian who had been *like maybe* a little bit of a confused hippy who had taken too much acid in the sixties! Not anyone's idea of a "normal" church minister.

I walked out on the platform that evening in front of a sea of believers and shared Roger's amazing story of conversion, complete with him hearing the voice of God. I brought him up with me on stage, and it blew his mind almost as much as God himself speaking from heaven! He gave his testimony and talked about his life change. He was filled with the Holy Spirit as he stood in front of the people. There was not one atom of his body that was not being touched by the supernatural resurrection power of Jesus Christ!

Roger moved into one of our houses. So many people were getting saved that we opened up multiple homes to rescue people. We gave the homes names like the Philadelphia House, Mansion Messiah, the House of Miracles in Santa Ana, and the Bluetop Motel in Newport Beach. Roger studied the Bible for at least a couple of years in our fellowship, until he grew in maturity and ventured back into society with a solid foundation in Jesus Christ.

I stand in total awe every time the Lord touches our lives, every time he reveals his loving-kindness toward us, every time he uses me. Believe me, I am the least likely candidate for what the Lord has done with me. I look back, now in my forties, and the only explanation I can offer is that since I was a little child, I have desperately needed God. I had nothing or no one to turn to except God. He responded to my cries with a plan and a divine purpose for my life!

TWO

Broken Foundations

BEFORE I EXPLAIN why I consider myself to be a totally unlikely candidate for what the Lord has done with me, let me tell you about a series of events that I think are quite significant. It might shed some light on the subject. People often write certain things off as mere coincidence—but not me.

Back in the mid-eighties, I was soon to be traveling to five countries. As our ministry team usually did, we organized a meeting for our upcoming journey. Two men of God were speaking at this particular missionary meeting, which took place in a borrowed church building in Santa Cruz, California. A lot of people came from several different fellowships, and the entire meeting was recorded.

One of the speakers was a man named Carl Gallivan from Peninsula Bible Church, a strong evangelical congregation in Northern California that I was associated with. When Carl started to speak, he said, "When I think about Lonnie Frisbee, I think about this scripture:

You are no better than the people of Canaan—your father must have been an Amorite and your mother a Hittite! When you were born, no one cared for you. When I first saw you, your umbilical cord was uncut, and you had been neither washed nor rubbed with salt nor clothed. No one had the slightest interest in you; no one pitied you or cared for you. On that day when you were born, you were dumped out into a field and left to die, unwanted. But I came by and saw you there, covered in your own blood, and I said [unto you], 'Live!'

11

That's the scripture he quoted. It is Ezekiel 16:3–6, and it concludes with: "I said unto you, 'Live!'"[3] I was slightly confused about what the speaker was saying, because I never considered myself to be along the lines of what he was reading.

The next day we were off on our mission trip, heading first to England, then to Israel, Egypt, South Africa, and Brazil. So after four or five hours of flying on the first leg of our journey, we landed in New York City at three o'clock in the morning. To add to our fatigue and mounting frustrations, there was absolutely no lodging available in New York City. Everything was booked. We scrambled around and finally got a hotel room in New Jersey at a Quality Inn. We were only going to be able to get around two hours of sleep at the most before we had to catch our international flight. We were exhausted.

So anyway, we arrived at the Quality Inn at four o'clock in the morning. Our room was long and narrow, musty from so many people staying there, and smelled of mildew. At the end of the room, I saw a Bible propped up. I went over and turned the light on. It was a Gideon Bible opened up to Ezekiel 16, the page dog-eared to the exact scripture spoken over me the day before in Santa Cruz. I mean, the Bible page was turned up, underlining the exact scripture!

My missionary partner said, "What do we do now, Lonnie? Get down on our knees and praise the Lord?"

We got the tape out from the day before and played it. As we listened, there in front of us was the Bible tilted up with the page folded to emphasize the exact text. It was powerfully supernatural. I felt like God spoke to me in an entirely different way than he had ever spoken to me before:

No one had the slightest interest in you; no one pitied you or cared for you. On that day when you were born, you were dumped out into a field and left to die, unwanted. But I came by and saw you there, covered in your own blood, and I said [unto you], 'Live!'

I'm not going to try to interpret it any more than is obvious. If you try to interpret it, the meaning gets taken away. This just hit me at a certain level in a very special way. God communicated something to me that he really wanted me to know, and in 1986, I definitely needed to know that. New Jersey is pretty far away from Santa Cruz, California, and the supernatural move of God's Spirit—well, it speaks for itself.

MY OWN STORY

So many people have differing opinions about me that I feel the Lord would have me tell my own story, starting with a short account of my bizarre childhood. I was born in the Santa Ana Hospital to Ray Frisbee and Janette Ashley on June 6, 1949. My father is a full-blooded American Indian—Cherokee and Choctaw. My grandfather lived on an Indian reservation. My father was a country-western entertainer who played in honky-tonks. He was a womanizer and an alcoholic. I often describe my biological father, Ray Frisbee, as a "Cherokee Indian honky-tonk singer with whiskey breath." My earliest recollection of Ray is of him singing Willie Nelson songs.

Besides the singing, one of my first childhood memories is of him beating my mother. As an infant, I recall him being very cruel to her, and there was a lot of screaming and crying. I could hear her from my crib. I know it was my baby crib, because I remember the bars on it. I often heard her screaming under the fist-popping blows of my father's dysfunctional life.

I also remember coming into the kitchen as a toddler and walking on

Ray Frisbee

shattered glass. Ray used to do things like break all the dishes and bust all the windows out of the house. A lot of it had to do with uncontrolled rage. He would break eggs on the ceiling. He would literally take raw eggs and throw them up on the ceiling, all while laughing hysterically. This was when he was drunk. One of his last girlfriends told me that she had to get a restraining order against my father. He had consecutively busted out every window of her house and, for the grand finale, put a kitchen chair through the television. He went through five sets of windows and a TV. He almost killed the woman, he beat her so badly. He brutalized all of the people who were in his life.

Now let me share a little about my mother and her side of the family. It's a little better by far. Several years ago, my grandmother, Naomi Ingler, invited me to a family reunion where I met about 115 of my relatives on my mother's side. Lo and behold, there's a family history of ministers that goes all the way back to Essex, England, during a revival that had taken place there way back when. There are ministers in the family line, itinerate ministers who traveled around and cared for different groups of people. I was very surprised to find out that I was this generation's minister in my family. Here I thought that I was just a burned-out drug addict the Lord found in the gutter. But it wasn't that way at all. It was heritage.

I had been fasting from public speaking during this period of my life, and the fast had gone on for quite a long time. However, the Lord told me that I could speak at my family reunion. I spoke on genealogies, and everybody cried.

My mother was sixteen years old when she married, and my dad was fifteen. They were young teenagers. So Ray Frisbee, my cruel father, was just fifteen years old when he married my mom. Nevertheless, that doesn't excuse any of his cruelties.

I remember him hitting my mother, saying, "How come you can't have whole babies?"—because my older brother and I were both born clubfooted. Ray used to beat my mother because she gave him two crippled children.

My left foot was a severe clubfoot, and if it hadn't been for the surgery done in 1950 to drop my underdeveloped Achilles' heel, I would have never been able to walk normally. I ended up having two major surgeries on my leg. The Old Testament says that a priest cannot be clubfooted,[4] so I'm a clubfooted New Testament priest, redeemed by a new order!

Having a handicap can really be a challenge, especially with other kids as you're growing up. Oh yeah, they singled me out right away. They beat me up. They called me names. They picked on Tiny Tim. I was a frail, sickly kid with a funny leg. I remember being beaten up on the way to school, and I remember being beaten up on the way home from school. It's just the way it was. It's "animal" what the children did to me. They persecuted my older brother also. They would yell at us and say, "Hey, pigeon toe!"

From left to right: Lonnie, Wesley, and Stan

I want everyone to know that I realize how cruel the children (as well as many adults and a school board) were to Ryan White, the champion of the straight boys with the plight of AIDS. I know how cruel the children were to Ryan White, because they were that cruel to me. But I praise God for that clubfoot—it separated me from the pack. Who would have wanted to be a part of their little cruelties, or more like *big* cruelties? They were little children with big cruelties. Not so much reflecting who they were, but who their parents were. Reflecting what mankind is at the core.

When I was three and a half years old, I was in downtown Santa Ana with my mom, dad, and brother Stanley. This is the first time I ever remember getting beaten by my dad. Like I said, I was just a toddler. We got out of the car, and there was a nicely dressed black

15

man in a suit and tie walking past. How could I ever forget the face of that man—because I said, "Look, Daddy," pointing my tiny little baby finger at him, "Look, Daddy! There's a nigger."

My father proceeded to take his belt off, take me by one arm, and beat the living daylights out of me with his belt, hitting me across the face and up and down my body. You know, I had absolutely no protection from what he was doing to me. I was three and a half years old! The man I called "Daddy" was beating me with a belt because I said, "There's a nigger." I'll never forget his bigotry and hypocrisy. He taught me the word and then beat me for it. He should have realized that somebody will always come along who is bigger, stronger, and meaner! Anyway, he traumatized me and bonded me to unnecessary brutality at a very early age. He seemed to enjoy beating his children. Or at least the ones he didn't think were his.

Ray always said he was sure I was not his kid. My mother had always been faithful in her marriage, while he had never been faithful to anyone. He had never been faithful to a wife and never been faithful to his children, which he boasts of fathering fifteen. Ray Frisbee was a mean and brutal man, and I feel sorry for people who are in personal prisons like the one he was in.

I was about four years old when my parents split up. Ray didn't want to pay child support for me, continuing to make claims that I was the milkman's son. In 1953, he wanted my blood tested to prove that I wasn't his kid. What a ridiculous thing anyway—he never paid child support for the sons he *knew* were his own, Stanley and Wesley. He was just making trouble.

One day we were in front of the courthouse in Santa Ana again, and my father was screaming and cussing under the influence of alcohol, telling my mother that I wasn't his. He was being very cruel with his words. And then they began to struggle over me. My mother had hold of my arm and was pulling on me while screaming and crying. That's one time I can vividly remember the whiskey breath of my father, the sweet whiskey smell. In fact, I don't remember ever being around my dad when he wasn't drunk.

So Ray grabbed hold of my other arm, and he and my mother had a tug of war over me. It felt like they were pulling my arms out of their sockets. It was very painful along with all the screaming and yelling and cursing. Then my father hit my mother hard enough to get me away from her. He dragged me down some flights of stairs and across a lawn, dragging me along faster than I could stay up with him—I was only four. He threw me in the car. I was screaming, and he hit me in the face. I wet my pants.

I truly hated my father ever since then. He hit me so hard in the face that I'll never forget the absolute terror and pain of that moment. It made my ears ring. I lost control of myself and went to the toilet in my pants. He was a cruel man. He bonded me to cruelty, to his violence. Ray Frisbee didn't want to pay child support for me, because he said I was a bastard. That's what he called me when he hit me. He said, "You little bastard."

Ray Frisbee also had a "keep them barefoot and pregnant" attitude toward women. He always had that attitude. While he was married to my mom, he had an affair with an ex-girlfriend from high school. My mother never liked to share about this, because she never wanted to dredge up the past. It was too painful. But let me dredge it up for her. Being victimized in a marriage where there is violence and severe beatings is absolutely devastating and unacceptable. People need to be rescued and healed.

One time Ray Frisbee beat my mother so badly that it closed both of her eyes until they were swollen like eggs. They turned black and blue and magenta and chartreuse. I remember the colors. He also took a pair of broken scissors and cut all of her hair off. That was pretty much the end of that, the final blow to the marriage.

Ray was already involved with this other woman when that happened, so he ran away from my mother with his old girlfriend and deserted his family. My mother was left with three babies and no financial support. Not that he ever really supported his family. All the money went to faster horses, younger women, and older whiskey. I think Tom T. Hall must have written that country-western song "Faster Horses" about my father—"*As he spit between his boots with tobacco-stained teeth.*"

COMPLICATED ROOTS

My family roots start to get very complicated about right here. Ray Frisbee ran off with his old girlfriend, a young married woman named Velma Graham. My mother was trying to chase down my dad for some food money because we had none. My great-grandmother allowed us to live in a shack behind her house in Orange, California. I remember the shack was covered with tarpaper and chicken wire and had a bare concrete floor.

Meanwhile, the husband of Velma Graham was also out looking for his wife while my mother, Janette, was looking for her husband. Oddly, in the pursuit of finding their mates, Lyle Graham and my mother found one another, fell in love, and were eventually married. Soon they had their *own* family with the birth of their sons Scottie and Stevie Graham. So I had two half brothers in this new family along with a new stepfather.

Then out of wedlock, Ray had two bastard sons by my stepdad's first wife, Velma. When Velma first hooked up with my dad, she already had a two-year-old named Larry. As the love affair increased, she just dumped Larry off with her mom and dad and never went back for him. The grandparents raised the child.

Velma lived together with my dad just long enough to reproduce their two illegitimate children. Ray always left babies crying at the door. He deserted every one of his women. He deserted every one of his children also, except for his only daughter out of the alleged fifteen offspring. But anyway, that's the gist of a pretty complicated family background. I have many half brothers and at least one half sister I never met.

Maybe you can start to get the picture of how all this was very traumatic to a little child, especially to an overly sensitive, sickly kid like me. But then, of course, when it rains, it pours. Sometime after my father left my mother, the three of us—Stanley, Wesley, and me—were dropped off at a strange home. It was so confusing to me, and I don't remember most of the details. It's almost like a foggy dream, but it was real.

I just remember my mom and stepdad taking us there, introducing us to these strangers, and then leaving. And that's where we lived for a while. I don't even know for how long. This was when the first abuse happened to me. An older boy stripped down a whole bunch of us children who were living there. We were forced to be in a doghouse naked, and some abuse took place. Like I said, I don't remember how long it was, but we lived there for a period of time while my mother and stepfather worked out their separate divorces and new marriage together.

By the way, the person my stepdad, Lyle, hated the most in the world was my biological father, Ray Frisbee, the man who took Lyle's first wife and had beaten his second. So he raised us three Frisbee boys in total rejection. At least that's how I felt. He was from a military background and was super strict. We could only call him by his first name. We were not allowed to eat a meal with my parents. In addition, our meals had to be consumed in total silence.

I loved my two new brothers, Stevie and Scottie, when they came along, but I could tell they were the **real** family in Lyle's eyes. I hated Ray, my natural father, for all of the physical abuse and for what he did to my mother, but as the years of criticism and emotional rejections from my stepfather started to pile on, I perfected my hatred for Lyle Graham as well. I desperately wanted his approval in the beginning and was starving for affection—but never got it. It seemed like my whole life was a series of disasters and rejections. I loved my mother, but she was reeling from her own problems and even had an emotional breakdown in the midst of everything she was going through.

And if you think that things couldn't get much worse, you're wrong! They definitely could—and did. For me it happened when I was eight years old. My parents often allowed a neighbor to babysit us. He was a high school senior, and he paid special attention to me. I really liked him. He played games with us and carried me on his shoulders. It all seemed so innocent, normal, and fun. Sometimes he would put me on his lap and read to me, and I remember him stroking my hair. It felt good to have someone show me any kind of personal affection.

But then it turned into a nightmare. One day he took me into the shower with him. He undressed us both, and in the shower he sexually molested me. I was this skinny little eight-year-old, and he was this huge seventeen-year-old. I was absolutely petrified.

After it was over, he bound me to secrecy, but I was so traumatized that I finally got up enough courage to tell my mother. My parents subsequently had a meeting with the babysitter's parents, and the adults finally concluded, "Lonnie is making it all up." Unbelievably, after a short time they even allowed this young pedophile to babysit us again.

When he got me alone, he asked, "Lonnie, why did you say those things about me?" He threatened me and molested me again and again over the next couple of years. I was absolutely terrified to tell anyone. No one believed me before, and no one could be trusted. I was filled with shame and guilt and confusion. A psychologist recently told me that when my parents didn't rescue me from the molestation as an eight-year-old child, it broke the foundations of my life.

THREE

A Pinecone Prayer

ONE OF THE BRIGHT spots in my young life was my grandmother Naomi. Thank God for her. She was a simple, uncomplicated lady. As I mentioned before, she was my grandma on my mother's side. She belonged to the First Christian Church and couldn't really conceive that there were any other kinds of believers other than First Christian. I loved her very much. She had a really strong interest in making sure that I attended Sunday school. She bought me all brand-new clothes, brand-new shoes, and a white shirt with a little bow tie. Then she marched me down to a little Pentecostal church, which was the closest church to my house, where the people would, you know—*"Shandala Shandi"*—speak in tongues and shout, "Glory, hallelujah!" and things like that. As a child, I thought it was radical and wonderful.

One day the church brought all of us children to a little puppet show. It was held in a Union Hall on Chapman Avenue in Orange, California. For the first time in my life, I really heard the gospel story. I heard how Jesus died for me and gave his life on the cross so that I could have eternal life. Suddenly I understood the significance of that event and went forward to the stage area at this little marionette puppet show. I got down on my knees and accepted Christ into my heart. I was eight years old, but I could still take you to the very spot in the very same building where it happened. I was born from above by the supernatural resurrection power of God. It is absolutely the greatest miracle anyone can experience, no matter what age!

The people at my grandma's church were very nice to me. They adopted me and put me in their Christmas pageant as one of the sheep. They even took me to a camp. They were really caring and devoted people. I love those bun-on-the-back-of-the-head, fanatical Pentecostals—and I am one. I see my heritage among the

Pentecostals. Not in the denominational category, but in the Spirit. I wouldn't want to call myself a charismatic or a Lutheran or a Quaker or anything like that. I'm Pentecostal because I waited on God and the power and anointing of the Holy Spirit fell on me, just like he will fall on every desperate and open heart. I qualified in that department and was born again at the age of eight years old. That was my call. Even though I didn't even begin to comprehend or understand much at the time, I just knew that something real and eternal had taken place—that Jesus loved me and was my friend.

Two weeks after I gave my life to the Lord, the babysitter molested me for the first time. I think it's significant that it happened two weeks after I became a Christian. The Bible says that the Evil One comes immediately and tries to snatch away what has been sown, to kill and destroy what has been planted. His messenger in my case was a neighboring predatory student. I was only eight years old, frail in body, often ill, with a crippled leg. I had bad tonsils and was just a sickly, little, skinny, innocent child. How diabolical the enemy is. The violation didn't keep me away from God, but it did mark my life with a deep wound that followed me like a living nightmare even as I followed the call of God for my life.

CAMP SEELY

Thank God for my grandma and the many other Christians who were placed in my life at strategic points to help rescue, nurture, and deliver me. It just so happened that right about the time when I was being molested as a child, my grandmother felt moved to pay for my way to camp. She heard about Camp Seely over the radio and made me a deal: "Lonnie, you pay half of your way to camp, and I'll pay the other half."

Well, I was off and running, washing windows, mowing lawns, and whatever else I could do. I jumped at the opportunity and raised half of the money, and my grandma paid the other half. Soon I was on my way to Camp Seely in the Crestline area of the local San Bernardino Mountains.

Full of nature in the beautiful surrounding mountain landscape, the camp was run by a man named Dr. William Ore, one of the men who had a great impression on my young spiritual life. He was famous in the church as a Bible teacher and a leader among the evangelicals. Dr. Ore was the one who would ding the little bell and sound like Santa Claus when he talked on the radio.

Upon arrival, to my surprise, I found out I was the only person from an unsaved family in the whole facility. And this wasn't a little camp either. It was huge. A large staff worked months in advance to provide a place in the mountains where kids could be introduced to the great outdoors and ultimately to the great King. Really, it's the best idea. I definitely think that people experience God at retreats in a very special way.

One of the rules at camp was that you had to shower every day. Back at home, the teenage babysitter was sexually molesting me, so when it was time to take a shower, I ran away and hid myself in a riverbed. There was a dry log and some tall grass there. From my hideout, I could hear: "Lonnie! Lonnie!" Everyone in my cabin was out searching for me, thinking that I was lost. They kept a "hawk eye" on all the children at camp.

Here I was, a little boy having to explain to the adults why I was hiding. I was forced to tell them that I didn't want to shower with anybody. They asked why, but I was too ashamed to tell them. They had no idea that I was being molested. They finally concluded that I was afraid to take a shower around all the other kids, so they had a young counselor take me by myself, which was the worst thing since it had all started in a shower with a young man who looked almost like the counselor.

However, every year the Lord would get hold of my heart at that camp so powerfully through the worship and the loving friendships. I met some of the most wonderful missionaries and some of the most dedicated Christians in the whole evangelical church. I heard stories about Jim Elliott, who, along with his entire missionary team, was slaughtered in the Amazon. *Through Gates of Splendor* by Elisabeth Elliot was written about those martyrs. Their deaths sparked a tremendous missionary surge in the fifties, as other Christians were touched and called to foreign shores.

To me, camp was like heaven. We would sing Christian songs, play games, and eat all our meals together with lively conversation. At home my brothers and I ate separately from the adults because Dad couldn't stand having kids at the table. We were raised in an atmosphere in which you couldn't make any noise at the dinner table. We had to eat our food and be QUIET! It wasn't until I was out of the house permanently as a teenager when I discovered normal people actually had conversation at the dinner table. And by the way, I never tasted fresh vegetables in my whole life either until I got out of my home. Everything we ate was out of cans.

But Camp Seely was another world. I won prizes in the talent show and was awarded a ribbon for the cleanest cabin in the camp. I became friends with everyone, and they considered me a part of their lives and families. They would put me on their laps and tell me stories about Jesus and things like that. Every year when camp was over, the leaders could not understand why this little boy was begging them, "Please don't make me go home! Let me stay here! I'll wash dishes, I'll work, I'll prove myself to you people!" I was too little to understand that they were all leaving. Nobody lived there.

Every year for the three or four summers that I attended Dr. Ore's camps, it was the same thing: "Please don't make me go home!"

"Well, Lonnie, don't you want to be with your mom and dad?"

"No!" I'd say, crying and ashamed and afraid I'd be rejected.

At the closing camp meetings, they would have what was called the "pinecone service." That's when we'd go out into the forest, find a pinecone, write down a prayer, and put it inside the cone. Then we'd build a huge bonfire. Not a normal camping bonfire, but a big, *huge* bonfire. It was a giant circle of flames built especially for the closing services of the camp. In my pinecone was a little prayer that said, "God, would you please save my mom and dad!"

The kids would all share something from their hearts at these closing camp meetings. At one particular closing service, when it came my turn to share, I began explaining to the entire camp that I wasn't from a Christian home, and I started to cry. I couldn't talk; I got totally choked up. Then I noticed that everybody was crying. It really affected me, and I always remembered that my words moved people to tears.

Every time I'd go back home from camp, I could only remain strong for five or six days, and then I was pulled back into the sexual molestation. Pretty bad, huh? No one can imagine the guilt or the shame or the fear unless they've also experienced it. The young pedophile tried to get inside my head and convince me that it was all "normal" and not to be afraid of him. Nevertheless, he would also force me to swear to absolute secrecy. When I would come back from camp, I would feel like I lost my relationship with God—because I couldn't be good.

MRS. BEARDSLEY

As I grew up in our dysfunctional blended family, I learned to somewhat adapt. I hid the dark, dirty secret about the babysitter. No one believed me anyway. I was so ashamed and afraid to say anything again. I learned the painful art of blocking and numbing. It was the unreal part of my existence, completely separate from the real, everyday stuff of life.

We had six boys in the family. My stepfather was a hod carrier, one of the hardest labor jobs in construction that anybody could ever do. He carried cement on his shoulder up ladders and scaffolds to the bricklayers. My stepfather was a hod carrier for nineteen years.

In the fifties we went through a recession, almost a depression. However, things picked up, and we eventually sold our house in the city of Orange and moved into a real nice home in Costa Mesa, California. After that move, we were raised in the Newport-Costa Mesa area of South Orange County for the rest of our young lives. I was in the third grade when we made the transition. I was also delivered from the molestation.

I knew that God was real from my experiences at camp and from my grandmother's church, so after the move, I got involved in a local church called Central Bible Church. It was a church that did not believe in water baptism for young people. They only believed in baptism for individuals who had reached a certain "age of accountability" and could understand what was going on. I asked for baptism, but they said I wasn't old enough yet. Still, I became very involved in the choir and was heavily involved in church as a young man.

In addition to singing in the choir every year, I attended the Bible Exchange program at my public school, which they don't allow anymore. It was like catechism. We met across the street from our elementary school in a trailer and studied the Bible. I was a very strong Christian convert and loved the music, but I envied the wholeness in some of the families.

At my church I had a blind choir teacher named Mrs. Beardsley. I grew to love her very much. I was more or less tone deaf. In fact, I could not carry a note, but I still sang real loud anyway. That blind teacher could *definitely* tell where I was. I'd sing super loud and off-key with my little choir outfit on. I was a pathetic little boy who needed tons of recognition—and there was never enough. Mrs. Beardsley eventually chose me to lead her around by her arm.

So I continued to be in junior choir and to attend church regularly. I'd go to the Sunday school classes, and then I would stay after class, sit in the front row of adult church, and listen to Pastor Gabler share his sermons and ideas about God. I was a little boy sitting in the front row of adult church. I didn't understand what was going on, but I loved hearing about Jesus and about the Bible. Even though I didn't understand a lot of it, some came back to me later. Like it says, God's word never comes back void.[5]

I remember going up to my blind choir teacher and saying, "Mrs. Beardsley! Mrs. Beardsley! If you only have Oral Roberts lay hands on you, you can get your sight!" And then I cried.

Mrs. Beardsley grabbed my hands and told me, "Lonnie, I want you to know something. I'm blind, and I don't really expect to get my sight. But you know what? The first face that I'm going to see will be Jesus'."

After I attempted to get my blind teacher healed by telling her about Oral Roberts, I went home and cried and cried on my parents' bed. When I look back over my life, I take note that I had enough guts even to mention, as a young boy, that God could heal my beloved teacher.

Little did anyone know that in my adult ministry I was going to become a faith healer and that the Lord was going to open the eyes of the blind! He did it in South Africa, making front-page news. I believe that God wanted to heal—and could have healed—my blind choir teacher way back when. Nevertheless, all of us who love the Lord, including Mrs. Beardsley, will someday see Him face-to-face!

FOUR

Reefer Madness

I WAS DEEPLY involved in church until around junior high school. Then I started to hear a voice say, "Church is for sissies." That's what I heard: "Church is for *sissies*." In my mind I was going, "Whoa!" So I'd go to church, and then I wouldn't go to church. And then I'd go to church, and then I wouldn't go for two Sundays. I'd go to church again, and the Sunday school teacher would say, "Lonnie, your attendance is not good. You're not going to get a prize. You're not going to get a big gold star next to your name! We're not even going to give you a little one! You need to get on the ball and start attending!" After that, I wouldn't go for three weeks, and then I'd show up again. I weaned myself off of Sunday school because I didn't think that junior high kids needed to go.

After all, we were getting hair on different places. I was also starting to become more interested in girls and dating. Church started to make me feel guilty, so eventually I dropped out altogether. I mean, this was the early sixties. Instead of going to church, I started to use drugs: drinking cough syrup, taking pills, dropping acid. I was dropping acid *WAY* before I was smoking pot. I remember we were at a party, and somebody took out a funny-looking rolled-up cigarette from behind his ear. He lit it up, coughed, and passed it around. I said to myself, "That must be marijuana—*gasp!* Oh no!" It made its way to me, and I passed it by. I wouldn't touch it, because it was the "devil's weed." I had seen *Darkness On Your Doorstep* and the infamous *Reefer Madness* shown in all the schools.

Let me back up and interject a little story about becoming a clubfooted dancer—it parallels the drugs. When I was a little boy, I loved and adored the Mouseketeer Club. One of the Mouseketeers was named Lonnie, and he spelled his name like I did. All of the kids on the show had their turtleneck sweaters along with little mouse ears. On each program they would have roll call, and the Mouseketeers would introduce themselves to a nationwide Walt Disney audience.

They would do things like announce, "Today is Circus Day," or "Today is Cowboy Day," and then they'd have roll call. When Lonnie would shout out his name, saying, "I'm Lonnie the Mouseketeer," I'd time it perfectly, jump up, and yell real **loud** along with the TV, *"I'm Lonnie the Mouseketeer!!"*

So I had a secret desire to be a Mouseketeer as a child, except that I was a clubfooted kid. The Mouseketeers sang and danced and did all kinds of choreographed entertainment, so when my parents would have company over, I would arrange the seating and put on a tap-dance show. I was a clubfooted tap dancer. First, I would apologize to my audience for not having two good legs. I had one good leg and a bad leg, so I'd try to tap-dance with my good leg in front of my parents' company. I did this all the time.

My parents would get embarrassed and say, "Sit down, Lonnie!"

"No, I'm not finished yet!" and then I'd tap-dance with my one leg some more. It was pathetic, very sad. They told me that I'd never walk normally, let alone dance. My answer was, "Ha ha! We'll see about that!"

SHEBANG

Now I'll fast-forward about a decade to when I was attending Corona del Mar High School, which happens to be Brooke Shields's former high school. A girlfriend of mine had sent in for tickets a whole year in advance to this famous dance show on television. It was live with Casey Kasem on his very popular *Shebang* daily show. The tickets finally arrived, and we went on the program.

My girlfriend was like a giant Amazon woman. She was literally almost twice as big as I was. My eye line came to her breast line, and so here I was dancing on a television show with this *huge* woman. Instead of throwing her around, she was throwing me around. Still, Casey and the producers saw me and decided that I had a lot of talent. By the way, at that particular time I didn't look like a hippy at all. I looked like Wally Cleaver. I had a letterman sweater, yellow cactus casuals, paisley underwear that showed through my pants, wingtip shoes, and I used half a can of hairspray on my squared-off-in-the-back, Papa Doo Run Run haircut. Let's not forget I was also fully anointed with an overflowing amount of Jade East.

Lonnie
Frisbee

So the producers and Casey Kasem pulled me aside and said, "You there! Have we got a drugstore success story for you! We're going to put you on everything." And they did. I became a regular dancer on the show. It was so cool.

The first project was with the televised Miss Teenage America pageant. They immediately made us guys up to look just like Casey. They put us in wardrobe and makeup. They French-razor cut our hair and provided all our clothing. We were dancing escorts for the pageant contestants. After that, I was put on the live dance show every day for a year and a half. They bought me a car. I was driving around in a snazzy little brand-new car at sixteen.

It was amazing to be on live television daily. They didn't videotape the program and play edited versions on TV. That came later. The show was broadcast on KTLA Channel 5. People recognized me on the streets. It made me "famous." It was like being a regular on *American Bandstand* back in Philadelphia with Dick Clark, except this was a local LA show. By the way, they recently did a 40th anniversary documentary of the entire history of KTLA. In the documentary they showed a segment featuring *Shebang* with me dancing in the film. So, "See, Mom and Dad: I *can* do more than just tap-dance with one leg!"

Anyway, back then we were like grown-up teenage Mouseketeers. The regulars on *Shebang* were included in all the dance contests, and we won all the prizes at all of Casey's shows. He would do huge dances in different venues with top-of-the-chart guest

31

stars. Casey would personally introduce each one of us from *Shebang*. We'd come out and do our dance routines. It was teenage paradise. I had an absolute ball.

Lonnie at sixteen

I definitely became starstruck because from the beginning I was amongst the most famous people in LA in the entertainment world. I was able to hang around and meet the 5th Dimension, the Righteous Brothers, the Doors, the Seeds, Jackie DeShannon, Dionne Warwick, and almost every popular rock 'n' roll singer in the world. When Sonny and Cher came on the television show, Cher was only nineteen years old. I felt like I had my foot in it all.

I remember when the Doors came on the show. Jim Morrison was so high that the producer said, "I'll never have this group back again." He didn't realize that the Doors would become one of the most famous groups in rock 'n' roll history. Nevertheless, the Doors were definitely messed up on psychedelics that day. They couldn't even begin to relate to what the crew and cameramen were telling them. They were absolutely blasted out of their heads.

The drugs also came into our lives during this same period, but not through the TV show. I mean, when I was doing the show, I didn't really have time to do drugs, especially during the week. I had high school, and then after school I'd drive from Corona del Mar to LA every day through the traffic to get to the Channel 5 studio to be on live television.

I also want to say that Casey Kasem really watched out for me. He was like a father figure and definitely cared for all the teenagers. He was also definitely straight, not gay. He fatherly watched over the young people on his television program. That's not the way it was with some other people who worked on the show. There were pedophiles everywhere, people who wanted, you know, fresh teenage meat. They were definitely there, but Casey was a good man and protected everyone.

The whole live television thing lasted for a year and a half. Eventually we started filming on videotape, but at first everything was live. I got used to the little red light going on and getting prepared for "action."

THE ACID TEST

Getting back to my introduction to drugs, like I said, I was terrified to try that "devil weed." Eventually in our society marijuana became the basic threshold drug, but it was a different process for me. By sixteen years old, I was dropping acid on the weekends and having all kinds of hallucinations. I got involved in a drug cult in Laguna Beach called Mystic Arts, which was part of a widespread organization of psychedelic acidheads under Timothy Leary and the Brotherhood. Different groups lived in Hawaii and in Laguna Canyon, while still others branched off and lived up in Silverado Canyon.

We had communities of people who believed in LSD as a religion. I turned on *hundreds* of people to drugs. I was definitely convinced and committed. I bought LSD with my own money and gave it to sixteen-year-old kids my age, to my older brother, my neighbors, people I went to school with, to anybody and everybody who wanted to turn on. I'd say, "Hey, you wanna drop acid with me this weekend?" And then we'd go out to wilderness places and all take LSD.

We dealt LSD to other high school kids and junior high kids. We sold vials of acid and four-way acid tabs that would put you on a twelve-hour psychedelic high you couldn't come down from even if you begged! That was one of the most important things, the main ingredient of the "acid test." The test was more or less, "Can you get in and can you get out?" Or as the Beatles wrote it: *"Turn off your mind, relax, and float downstream. It is not dying."* You know, turn off your mind and find the meaning of love.

So we were all caught up in the belief that LSD was the answer. That LSD was God. All of us thought the same way. I questioned my former personal experiences with God. As a group of young people, we became naturalists and nudists. We gave up eating meat and were involved in orgies. Everybody slept with one another and lived in communes from time to time. We were persuaded that drugs were going to show us a different way from the materialistic Orange County culture we had been raised in all our lives. And guess what? They did!

But then, of course, drugs really did destroy a lot of my friends. Some are in institutions. They took acid one time—or one time too many—and were gone. It was like a magical blank slate. They took a tab of acid, and it made the slate go clean. It wiped away all their memories, and they had to be put in mental institutions. They didn't pass the acid test.

SOUTHEAST ASIA

Vietnam was going strong during this same time frame. Vietnam was a literal drugstore of heroin, opiates, and everything else. The shelves of that dangerous store were extremely well stocked with a very heavy ganja type of Asian marijuana, various brands of psychedelics, uppers, downers, mixed in with crates and boxes of amyl nitrites, which the army used for battlefield shock and battle fatigue. They would put poppers under the soldiers' noses. There were more drugs in Vietnam than there were in California by far.

So the kids over there in Vietnam were getting killed by the thousands, while we were protesting at home, dropping acid, going out into the desert on weekends, taking every kind of drug we could get our hands on, including peyote. And all of this was happening while we were searching and trying to figure out life in general. It was a crazy time.

Being half American Indian, I discovered that taking peyote for an American Indian was legal, at least at that particular time. We subsequently found out where they grew peyote in New Mexico and eventually acquired a regular source of peyote buttons. We tried different varieties of hashish from India and Pakistan, you know, *"feel the texture of the material."* We also found out what psychedelic mushrooms looked like, and someone lined up an excellent supply of "magic mushrooms." California was the hot spot, the place to be if you were young and wanted to "turn on and tune in."

The sixties were definitely a radical time with a lot of bad happening—but not all bad. We were honestly searching and experimenting. We were a rebellious generation looking for love and purpose and meaning. We explored other religions and belief systems. We wore Indian bedspread guru shirts and beads, went barefooted or wore sandals. We were into art, music, and poetry. In many ways, it was the beginning of a glorious renaissance in our own generation. But for far too many, it was the beginning *and* the end.

FIVE

Haight-Ashbury

AFTER THE COMPLETELY radical year and a half of live television, the TV dance show *Shebang* began shooting video instead of continuing live. Things were changing in broadcasting, and things were definitely changing for me. I went off to college in late 1966, way up north in San Francisco. Subsequently, I moved to the Haight-Ashbury during the much-publicized Summer of Love in 1967. I lived right in the midst of it all. It was a totally amazing time in my life and a totally radical chapter in contemporary American history.

MY ART

Previously, I had won a scholarship from the Boys Club of America. A wealthy Jewish man had lost his fourteen-year-old boy in a drowning accident at the Boys' Club in New York City. This man put millions of his dollars into a scholarship fund for talented boys. It was for things like violin, classical piano, and art. Ironically, when I was fourteen years old, a neighbor lady submitted my portfolio, and I won one of these Julius David Epstein scholarships.

I was so thrilled to have my artwork recognized. The scholarship began by putting me into adult art school at the age of fifteen. I attended the School of Art and Design in Laguna Beach for a year and a half on weekends and at night. This award eventually brought me

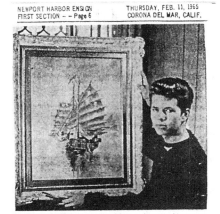

THE PAINTINGS of Lonnie Frisbee, 14-year-old student at Corona del Mar High School, are on view during February in a one-man show at the Costa Mesa Savings & Loan gallery. Lonnie, son of Mr. and Mrs. Lyle Graham, 215 Cecil Pl., Costa Mesa, won top honors at the age of 7 at the Laguna Beach Art Festival and recently won honorable mention in the Westcliff Art Show, competing with more than 200 adult artists. His versatility includes being a finalist in a cake baking contest at the Orange County Fair, winning dance trophies, and competing on the junior varsity wrestling team at Corona del Mar High School.

to one of the most exciting art schools in the country—the Academy of Art University in San Francisco.

At seventeen I dropped out of high school and enrolled in the art college. One of my high school teachers had previously moved up north and helped me get accepted into the college. I lived with this family in San Francisco when I first arrived. People don't know this about me, but I want to remind them that I was not a hippy-hobo-freak when I arrived in the Haight-Ashbury. I was a letterman in high school wrestling.

I was a clean-cut kid. I had what I considered to be good morals from my church background even though I had been experimenting with drugs, sex, and rock 'n' roll. Nevertheless, I had a genuine love and concern for people. The seed that God birthed in my heart at age eight was definitely still there.

ARTIST WINS — Lonnie Frisbee, 18, is congratulated by Boys' Club director Lee Vanhorn after winning a Julius Epstein Foundation scholarship in art. In background is one of his paintings.

Mesa Youth Knows

Art Lessons Not Important

Lonnie Frisbee never had a Steven David Epstein Foundation lesson in art, but you'd never know it to look at his paintings.

Soon, however, the 18-year-old Costa Mesa youth will have at least $552 worth of lessons from the instructor of his choice.

Frisbee, son of Mr. and Mrs. Lyle Graham, 215 Cecil Place, was named winner of arts.

Established by Julius in memory of his drowning victim, the fund is administered th...

Renewals of the grant a considered if the boy satisfactory progress.

Lonnie will begin his teacher has been chosen addition to his regular work, Vanhorn stated.

THE COMMUNITY

It just so happened that in 1967, major things were brewing on the West Coast of America right where I landed. It broke out in Golden Gate Park in "the Haight." This suburb of San Francisco is actually named after the intersection of Haight and Ashbury Streets. Some called the ensuing season of

38

Americana the "Haight-Ashbury movement," but it has lots of other names and labels. I moved to "the community" as soon as I could, where the rent was cheap (but not anymore!). I gravitated from my teacher's place, moved to the Haight, and rented a place of my own. I lived right in the midst of it all, right off Masonic Street.

I often saw Janice Joplin with her seven dogs walking down the streets of the Haight-Ashbury, with her long black velvet cape flowing behind her in the wind. If you tried to get an autograph from that woman, you would get attacked by her dogs. I also often saw Jimmy Hendrix, George Harrison, Jerry Garcia, and even Charles Manson.

This radical district of San Francisco became an absolute mecca for movements. Trends were being birthed almost on top of each other. In Golden Gate Park young people flocked to mammoth concerts. You could experience electric psychedelic bands like the Grateful Dead, who allegedly distributed LSD in Kool-Aid to a concert of eighty thousand people. You could hear Big Brother and the Holding Company, Santana, and Jefferson Airplane with, you know, *"One pill makes you larger, and one pill makes you small, and the ones that mother gives you don't do anything at all."* And so we were in a neighborhood full of psychedelic colors, magic and sorcery, and all kinds of counter-cultural rebellion.

Anton LaVey opened up the Church of Satan in the neighborhood and allegedly revised the Satanic Bible while there. He laughed at society, and society laughed back, asking the bald-headed, black-robed priest, "Do you *really* believe in the devil?" It was reported that he wrote the Satanic Bible, not by inspiration from Satan, but for money at the request of Avon Books.

He had people like Jayne Mansfield in his church. By the way, Sammy Davis Jr. and other famous people were also really into satanic things under his banner. People were tattooing "666" on their right hands or on their chests. People were even shaving their heads, marking "666" on their hairlines, and then letting their hair grow back over their own personal "mark of the beast." It was wild and very dark.

The New Age movement also had many of its roots in the Haight-Ashbury. People were calling everything that was happening the "Age of Aquarius." We also had the overall flower power, peace-loving, dope-smoking, acid-dropping, long-haired hippy movement. In addition, the anti-war movement, the gay rights movement, and the Jesus movement all began here. The Black Panthers even had a presence.

The feminists also developed in the Haight. At first, you couldn't be a part of the women's rights movement unless you had tits. Some of the first feminists didn't want any men in the women's movement. Later it became *okay* for a male to relate to the feminist movement. Maybe some of the rank and file encouraged their significant others to ease up on those of us with higher testosterone levels. Anyway, I truly am a women's libber. I think women should have every equal opportunity in life—in careers, in finances, in the expression of artistic ability, in every arena of our society. Who are we to say that women are lesser if they can do the same job just as well or maybe even better? It's like that bumper sticker says: "The best man for the job is a woman."

So here I was, getting quickly and completely caught up in the wild, rebellious, but exciting atmosphere all around me. My hair

grew longer and longer, and my style changed. I might have gone in looking like a seventeen-year-old preppy, but believe me, I came out looking like our friend Paramahansa Yogananda: *"I'm so pretty, oh so pretty, I feel pretty and witty and—'feel the texture of the material.'"*

My pompadour morphed into extremely long hair, I grew a full-length beard and wore beads, bells, robes, and sandals. Let's not forget the flowers in my hair. Wally Cleaver definitely came out looking like a guru. In fact, I looked like a skinny Catholic Jesus or maybe Isaiah's grandson.

After I became a long-haired hippy "freak," a lot of rednecks and mainstream citizens accused me of being a homosexual. It was true that I had been sexually victimized and somewhat indoctrinated as a child. However, the gay movement scared me. The gay men I saw in the Haight-Ashbury were way over the top. They fixed their hair up in these fabulously high, curly, bleached hairdos that went *up, up, up* and then flowed down around their scruffy black beards. They strutted down the street with one another, wearing hot pants and high heels and sometimes even making crude gestures as they marched past society. I said to myself, "Nah, I'm not going in that direction." I had seen enough of the homosexual world—from pedophiles coming after children, to the militant activists boldly marching down the streets of America—to realize that it is a dark, deceptive world and a very powerful counterfeit.

But in other ways for almost the entire first year of living on my own, I went wild. I started searching and experimenting like everyone else. I listened to many voices and philosophies and opinions. We all smoked dope, dropped acid, and tried almost every drug on the streets. A couple of times we went to the desert looking for UFOs. I even thought I saw one, but it was probably just trails from a recent LSD trip.

I loved my life in the Haight. There were a lot of teahouses in the community that I really enjoyed, the kind of hippy teahouses where people would sit around, drink tea, read poetry, and philosophize about the new revolution. We as a generation were being set free. We talked about our diets, clothing, hair, politics, and everything else—"Power to the People!"

TAHQUITZ CANYON

In the middle of all this excitement, I still missed my friends and family, and as the months rolled by, I'd occasionally hitchhike back down to Southern California. All the young people back home were continuing to turn on to drugs, protest the war in Vietnam, and search for answers. We loved to go to Tahquitz Canyon up near Palm Springs, get nude, and seek God. One time about a hundred of us—guys and gals—were arrested for being nude and smoking dope. They hauled us away stark naked in vehicles. It was crazy but definitely thrilling.

In spite of the many highs, I was still troubled. I felt a destiny surrounding me, but was, at the same time, confused about life and death, and even questioned the existence of any particular spiritual reality. Who **really** knew the truth? I remembered from my church background that Jesus claimed to be the truth. I had definitely felt the presence of God when I asked Christ into my life as a child. I also felt his presence at the summer camps, but it still seemed pretty bold for Jesus to say things like, "I am the way, the truth, and the life. No one comes to the Father except through me," or "I am the good shepherd who lays his life down for the sheep," or "I am the door."[6] (Sorry Jim, but you have *major* competition.) I was definitely confused but very open and honestly seeking. I would wonder, "How does it all fit?"

One day I was up in the canyon again by myself. It was a real hike back on the Tahquitz Canyon Trail. There is a beautiful stream and waterfalls along the way, and it is such a cool place. I finally arrived at one of my favorite spots. I took off all my clothes and literally screamed up to heaven, "Jesus, if you are really real—reveal yourself to me!!!"

Suddenly the whole atmosphere began to change around me. It began to tingle and shimmer and glow. I thought, "Uhh–ohhh! I don't even want to be here!" I was scared and shocked, positive it was not an LSD flashback. I didn't hear an audible voice, but I knew that I was in the presence of God Almighty. Then I saw a radiant vision, clear as crystal. I saw thousands and thousands of young people at the ocean lined up in huge crowds along the coast, going out into the water to be baptized. I could see it! I knew instantly that Jesus was real and that he was calling me to follow him. As the Lord lifted up my eyes, I saw a harvest field of people. They were like a huge wheat field. I saw in the vision thousands of people in the valley of decision.

The power of the Holy Spirit surrounded me from within and without. Then I saw a light from heaven come down and ordain me, and I could hear him say, "Go in my name, for I have touched your lips with a coal of fire that burns ever before the presence of God. Proclaim to the people that I am coming soon."

It was the most radical moment of my life. At eighteen years old, I was being called by God to serve him. It blew my mind, but I definitely said, "Yes, Lord!"

I came off that mountain a different person. I still didn't have all the answers, but I knew for sure that Jesus was real. He had responded to my desperate cry. I had an instant revelation of my calling. What a privilege, what a high calling, to be used by a loving God, a God who loved us so much that he died on a cross to save us from destruction, to save us from ourselves. All the scriptures from my childhood started to kick in and take on new meaning with revelation and life. I realized that the written Word of God was true and supernatural. God was invading my life, and it was so powerful and absolutely wonderful. I didn't need drugs anymore!

Back home, my friends and loved ones soon said that I was mad, but I was *struck* and had to obey. I immediately went to the beaches and preached. I would go to the teen dances where I used to go raise hell, and now proclaim that Jesus was Lord and that he was coming back. I could hear the young people my same age laughing and saying, "Let's go out at break time and hear Lonnie talk about God. Did you hear that Lonnie overdosed and had a nervous breakdown?"

As I continued to be faithful, the Lord slowly brought the vision about. One believed, then two, then five, then ten, then there were fifty, and then there were a hundred people coming to know Jesus at every single meeting I preached in. There came a day down the road a little when thousands came to the beach at Corona del Mar to participate in mass baptisms in the ocean, catching the attention of the whole world—**exactly** like the vision I saw.

NOVATO

I hitched back to the Haight-Ashbury on fire for God. After school, I would go into the community and witness for Christ, trying

43

to find people who would listen to what I had to say, because I knew I had to get out there and be a worker for God. One day I was in a favorite teahouse sharing my heart out about Christ when, to my surprise, I found a group of men standing around me, really listening to me like they were very interested in what I was saying. They seemed to be men at least in their thirties. I think I had just turned eighteen.

I should mention that I was still slightly confused with my doctrine as a young believer. You know, Scripture says, "You will know the truth, and the truth will set you free,"[7] but that's not instantaneously done in a little prayer. So I was carrying on about opinions that I had. It was a mixture of Christianity and Rainbow. The Rainbow movement, a vague blend of Timothy Leary's LSD cult and the "free love, world peace" hippy philosophy, caught people off guard, and all that Rainbow from the pit stuff can really confuse people. But anyway, after I finished sharing, this group of men started talking to me.

One of the men introduced himself as Ted Wise. He explained that they had a mission in the Haight-Ashbury. He encouraged me to come around. As we continued to talk, he invited me to come to dinner with them. They had a farm out in Novato where they worked for the Lord every day. It was very attractive to me to hear that there were people in the neighborhood who loved the Lord. So I met with this group of radical Christians at their place in Novato, which is about twenty-nine miles north of San Francisco. There were four families and eight children who lived community-style in an old farmhouse. It was a group of ex-LSD freaks who were definitely born again and had stopped taking heavy drugs.

Before the meal that first day, we joined in a circle to bless the food. Everything was homemade and nicely prepared. There was fresh bread and absolutely delicious home cooking from loving wives. In addition, I had a little mind-blowing experience in that kitchen, because it was the first time I ever felt the power of God in my body. As we stood and held hands in that family circle, asking the blessing over the food, I could feel an electric current flowing through my hands. It was the very first time I ever felt the presence and power of God in such a wonderful way. I took it as a sign from the Lord that he wanted me to be with these people. They asked me what I was doing with my life. I told them that I was in art school, but that I liked what I felt there with them.

One of the sisters said to me, "We don't mind if you come and live with us."

Believe me, that's exactly what I wanted them to say. That's what I *needed* them to say. I was lost and needed a family, a real family experience that I never got growing up in my extremely dysfunctional one. So experiencing God's family was really very appealing to me. They moved me in and accepted me in the clan.

I immediately named the ranch house the House of Acts. Like it says in Scripture: "Now all who believed were together, and had all things in common, and sold their possessions and goods, and divided them among all, as anyone had need."[8] That is a description of the early Christian movement living in community. We would read it together—and then we would *do* it!

And so the Lord locked me into this Christian commune. He had me experience life like I had never experienced life before. It was truly a blessing to be around these older men who were being such good examples and around loving marriages that functioned and didn't fall apart. I was extremely surprised that every married couple in the world didn't fight like cats and dogs, as I was exposed to some normalcy for the first time in my life.

It was a very sophisticated group of adults living at our old vineyard house. They were mostly from Sausalito, California, and they all felt a need to drop out of society. Like I mentioned, these were men and women in their thirties. All of them had been very successful. The husband of one family, Steve, was one of the greatest radio disc jockeys in the whole country. He was probably the highest paid AM disc jockey. One day at his station, he testified that "you must be born again." He was fired because he mentioned Jesus over the air. Ted Wise was a sailmaker and an artist. Every one of them had been into the drug culture but had come to a saving faith in Christ, and so the five different families sold all their possessions and moved into a community house in Novato, California, in 1966.

45

Another family moved in around the time I did. We raised the children all together in a regular hippy-type kibbutz. It was wonderful.

At one point David Wilkerson, author of the very popular *The Cross and the Switchblade* about Nicky Cruz, came with a production team to film our household for a documentary. I was eighteen years old in that movie, which was financed by the Assemblies of God denomination. They gave us a small amount of money and had us sign away our rights. They filmed everything. It was supposed to be a story of redemption about our efforts to reach people with the message of Christ. However, they named the film *The Runaway Generation*, and it was very negative. In fact, it was an *extremely* negative film. They misunderstood what we were all about, but we still had nothing but love for them.

GREAT REWARD

I withdrew from art school shortly after moving to Novato. I remember going to my locker with Steve, the former radio disc jockey from the House of Acts. He went with me to back me up. The principal of the Academy of Art University in San Francisco walked up to me and said, "Look it, Lonnie. I beg you—don't do this. Don't run with these men! You're going to be so sorry! You're only eighteen years old. You have a multi-thousand-dollar scholarship. You can even go to art school in Europe on this. It's a big chance for somebody who can't pay for school. You're making a big mistake. Don't do this!"

But then I heard a "still, small voice" say to me, "Lonnie, if you do this, there will be great reward, because I'm telling you to do this. You're not manufacturing this in your own mind. I'm telling you to do this. Clear out your locker, get out of here, serve me, and later on I'll bless you as an artist."

The principal of the Academy of Art really begged me. He walked me to the door after I cleared out my locker, then finally said, "When you walk out of here, it's over, buddy."

Nevertheless, I had this strong assurance inside of me that I was doing the right thing. My college days were over, but divine guidance kicked in as I focused on the Lord. I became dedicated to Romans 8:14: "For as many as are led by the Spirit of God, they are the sons of God." Once I made this decision, my life began to take on new meaning. The Haight-Ashbury was my launching pad!

So to make it a wrap—this radical season of my life has been etched into my heart forever. I love the cutting edge. I love over-the-top experiences, and it was one after the other. I love the people in the community even if many are confused and misguided. They were for real and all of us were basically searching. People called us long-haired, dope-smoking freaks. We even called each other freaks.

But of all the radical movements that were birthed in the Haight, what ultimately attracted me was the Jesus movement. From the beginning, I was looking for truth and love and reality. Jesus demonstrated his reality to me over and over, calling me, commissioning me, and sending me out. If I am truly any sort of freak, then I wholeheartedly choose to be a Jesus freak!

SIX

The Living Room

I WENT INTO the ministry full time at the age of eighteen with
the help of these brethren, mostly Ted Wise. After completely
dropping out of the Academy of Art University in San Francisco, I
joined the ranks of my new fellow soldiers of Christ, and we worked
the streets. We rented a place in the community, which we named
the Living Room. Something spiritual was being birthed beyond our
awareness, beyond our comprehension. But we felt the hand of God
leading and guiding. We fed people and ministered to them. It was
our local "mission," supported by Ed Plowman, the editor of the
magazine *Christianity Today*. We would lead people to Christ and
then bring them home. It was wonderful!

We were a team of five men who worked the Haight-Ashbury
every single day, five days a week. Our mission at the Living Room
was also like a hippy soup kitchen, which kept us extremely busy. It
was "soup, soap, and the gospel," just like General Booth set up in
England in the birthing of the Salvation Army. Only our version was
quite different. We had pillows thrown all over the place. Everything
was super casual and comfortable.

Our place was filled with hungry people—spiritually hungry and
physically hungry. The wives would go to the supermarkets and get
throwaway vegetables, which were fresh with maybe a few bad
marks, and they hit the bakeries to get "stale" bread that was dated
but still very good. We fed the poor with throwaway food. At our
ranch the women would lovingly clean up the vegetables and make
soup. We would have boxes and boxes of bread and other prepared
food, and then we'd drive for an hour from Novato into the Haight-
Ashbury. At the Living Room, we would pray together, have a Bible
devotion, and then go out in teams like the God Squad or the Blues
Brothers. We were on a mission from God long before John Belushi
ever thought so.

49

Like I said, we got the concept for the Living Room of "soup, soap, and the gospel" from General Booth, the man who established the Salvation Army. We saw how he rewarded his followers by giving them higher ranks and dressing them up in uniforms. Well, that was not us. We clearly saw that getting dressed up in uniforms wasn't what we were called to do, 'cause we were definitely non-conformists all the way. Every one of us dressed differently. We had different hairstyles and clothes.

We led this one guy from Boston to the Lord, and he had an *outrageous* Afro. You know, it shamed Angela Davis! It was huge. I personally wore Indian half robes and sometimes carried a staff. I had an animal-skin satchel (kind of like Johnny Appleseed). I carried my Bible in it and a wine bottle full of oil—virgin olive oil from the Holy Land with frankincense, myrrh, cinnamon sticks, and witch hazel. It was my secret biblical anointing oil with a cork in it. Whenever people would listen to me and I'd win a convert, I would pray for them and then—pull the cork. I was *very* generous with the anointing oil. I poured it on.

When I went out, I wore a deerskin cape with a painting of Jesus on the back of it. I had these neat animal-hair Indian moccasins that laced way up. I wore beads. You know, hippies like to wear a lot of jewelry and like to be "hip." There was a definite movement of fashion in the Haight-Ashbury and a movement of nutrition as well. There was a renaissance of folk music and folk dancing along with a renaissance in food, philosophy, religion, and everything else you could think of. The hippy movement liberated our *boring* polyester society. Even though it took a few wrong turns, I'm not sorry that I was in it.

One day Charles Manson started coming to our mission. I remember him telling people that he was Jesus (*not the Jesus I know, dude!*). Anyway, he was sloppy with his soup. It was getting in his beard, but he didn't care.

I said, "Hey, you're getting soup in your beard."

He said, "Dinner."

He was an obnoxious man. He said he was the devil. So one minute he was Jesus and the next he was the devil. He would come in, and as he was wolfing down bowls of homemade soup from the women, he would put us down for what we were doing in the community. Of course, this was while he was enjoying our delicious soup! So anyway, Manson would come into our mission, eat our food, and mock us.

STRAIGHT MINISTRIES

Also in the neighborhood were people from Campus Crusade for Christ and other Christian groups as well. Once our ministry really got rolling, we noticed that other ministries were dying. We would go visit Campus Crusade for Christ at their location. We'd knock on the door and then finally hear the latches come off—*latch, latch, latch, latch*. They'd open the door a little crack and say, "What do you want?" We would be standing there, and we were, you know, we were flower children. We looked like all of the hippies, and these "straight" Christians were cracking the door and saying, "What do you want?" They were afraid for their lives. You couldn't *be* in that neighborhood and be afraid, because the people would see it. You know, gangs would see it. Black panthers would see it. You could *not* be afraid. You had to walk down the street with a big happy smile on your face, because there were criminals and big drug dealers and whatever. The ministries were terrified. I mean, the straight ministries were terrified.

And then we had the Clayton House, a Christian community that was led by Dick Keyes. They were also a straight ministry that, I have to admit, did somewhat of a good job for the Lord. However, Dick Keyes was Assemblies of God, and he was very, very straight. There was not a "hip" bone in his body. When Dick Keyes would get converts, he would make them look like squeaky-clean Mormons. When you see two clean-cut, short-haired kids riding by on bikes, with ties on that are out of style—that's what Dick Keyes did to every one of his converts. He made them get short haircuts, poured Vitalis all over their heads, and then he put 'em in three-piece polyester suits. When they sat down in restaurants, they'd slide right onto the floor. You could see them coming like a total Haight-

Ashbury contradiction, an enigma. You'd see former hippies walking down the street in polyester suits with short haircuts, going, "What happened to me?"

We would do things like go over there and wash our brothers' feet. Our elder persuaded us that this was what the Lord wanted us to do. We would go and wash the feet of the Clayton House members to show humility, unity, and love. However, they had a very difficult time with us. They believed that you should be completely straight when you come out of the drug culture. We would read scriptures to them like: "Abide in the calling whereby you are called,"[9] but apparently Dick Keyes could not see past the hair. Still, I have to give him credit for being a *major* leader in the Jesus movement. The Clayton House was one of the starting places.

So there were many ministries that came into the Haight-Ashbury. The difference between them and us was that we were born out of the cow manure. We were that blade of grass that came up through a crack in the concrete—because we had to have the sun. We saw ministries come and go, but the whole time that the Haight-Ashbury movement was in its thrust, in its heyday, God put the glory of his Holy Spirit on us.

We went to different neighborhoods and made friends. We fed the poor and helped the totally drug overdosed by taking them home, bringing them into our house, and ministering to them the love of God. Billy Graham taught in his crusades that there are four things necessary for a well-balanced and established walk: prayer, fellowship, Bible study, and evangelism. God can put more of an emphasis on one aspect and then later come along and teach you about one of the others. He brings a balance into our lives so that ultimately the love of God is proven true in us: "If we say that we love God, but hate our brother, how dwelleth the love of God in him."[10]

Someone might say to his brother, "Be warm, be filled, be comforted," while that brother is suffering for his daily need. It would be a sin to pronounce that kind of a shallow blessing and not meet the need. We in the Haight-Ashbury were sincerely trying to bind up the brokenhearted and preach the good news. Ours was a gospel of rolling up your sleeves and getting to work. Like Arsenio Hall says, "Let's get busy!" I've always found it easier to slow something down than to start something up when it's dead cold.

Because we related so much to the people, we were able to reach many of the totally unreachable. We did things like rescue a fifteen-year-old girl who had been gang-banged by seven to nine large men who had given her LSD. That is one situation I remember well. The girl was completely crazed on acid. The men all had sex with her, and she was a fifteen-year-old runaway! We took her home and cared for her. She needed major healing, as the rapes and the LSD severely damaged her. Unfortunately, one day she was up in a tree in our backyard looking at a caterpillar when the film crew from David Wilkerson's ministry documented our communal home. The cameraman looked up and was slightly shocked to discover the young girl didn't have any underwear on. They accused us of having orgies and whatnot. It wasn't true.

Still, we did have our weaknesses. We would usually go out into the community in pairs. If, however, people in our household went out alone, sometimes they would take drugs. It was a really strong weakness. We finally got to the place where we would never go out alone. If some of us went out and got isolated by the people we were trying to help, sometimes those people offered up LSD—everybody had LSD—or they got us stoned on hash or something like that. I mean, I'm being honest. We were just coming out of the drug culture. It took a long time to *eventually* come out and completely not do it at all. It was the sway of Christianity that drew us out of decadence, immorality, and drugs. The more we helped other people, the stronger we got, and there became more of a necessity to set a good example. Believe me, God knows how to deliver, because he dearly, dearly loves each of us!

"BRINGING IN THE SHEAVES"

One of the most exciting times that I ever had when I first began to preach the gospel and one of the most precious early recollections of my calling was when I discovered this little Pentecostal grandma and grandpa couple in "the neighborhood" one afternoon. They were in their sixties and on a street corner boldly preaching.

This couple had a little fuzzy megaphone that made all these funny, weird noises with a lot of crackling and static when they talked through it. It would run out of batteries and things like that, but they had it all together. They would play a little bit of music and sing a hymn, standing right next to their bus with stickers and scriptures written all over it. They were hardcore Pentecostals, and they came into the Haight-Ashbury talking pure gospel, you know, shouting, "Love the Lord!" and "Jesus is the answer!" They were open-air preaching, and I never saw anybody do that before, 'cause I was from Orange County. I was sheltered. This was something you might see in places like downtown LA at the bus station.

So there I was, living in the Haight-Ashbury and watching this couple. I went up to them after they finished preaching and said, "I want to help you. I want you to teach me what to do, because I don't know what to do." I thought these people knew what they were doing.

They said, "Well, son, why don't you join us tomorrow down at Market Street, because we always work different neighborhoods. Meet us on Market Street right where the cable car turns around at two o'clock."

The next day I took the bus over there and, sure enough, they were right on time. God's servants being faithful to do what they felt called to do. However, to my shock and amazement, they put a sandwich board on me. It went over my neck and read: REPENT, THE WORLD IS COMING TO AN END!" JOHN 3:16 . . . "FOR GOD SO LOVED THE WORLD THAT HE GAVE HIS ONLY BEGOTTEN SON!" It was all written in bright red enamel-dripping paint.

Here I was, eighteen years old with a sandwich board on, standing there like in the old-time hymn: *Bringing in the sheaves, bringing in the sheaves. We shall come rejoicing, bringing in the sheaves!"*

I mean, I had a sandwich board on with red paint-dripping scriptures, thinking, "Oh my God! Oh my God! Is this it? This might definitely be the end of the world!"

The old man was speaking into the megaphone. You could hardly hear or understand him. Probably back in '67, they didn't make megaphones that well. Nevertheless, he preached his heart out for quite a long time. Finally, the man said, "Lonnie, now it's your turn." He and his wife took the sandwich board off of me and handed me the megaphone. I went to town. I didn't know what to do, so I started tap-dancing with one leg. Then I said to the people, "I have something that I want to say to you," and a crowd of people stopped on Market Street and started listening to me. It was my first time sharing Christ that I ever felt that special feeling from a crowd of people. When the old man and his wife were talking, people continued to walk by on the street, but when I started to speak, a large crowd formed. Soon I was in the middle of it, preaching the gospel under the anointing of the Holy Spirit, and people were interested in hearing what I had to say.

Then the old man said, "Son, you're an evangelist."

"What's an evangelist?" I was kind of like an airhead, an Orange County brat.

"Well, it's somebody who leads people to Christ. We all need to share our faith, but there are also special callings. It's a gift in the ministry, and you have it."

I was barely eighteen years old on Market Street with a sandwich board and a megaphone. It's a special memory for me, and it really brings me back to my roots. I was willing to do anything at all to improve myself as a soul-winner.

My street-preaching debut with this fanatical couple came early in my evangelistic career during my time in the Haight-Ashbury. God stamped that positive bond I felt with the crowd that day into my spirit, into my very soul. I knew for sure that I could reach people for my Lord, and I was propelled forward with energy, excitement, and determination to make my life count for Jesus. I had a supernatural revelation of the price he paid to free me. Who else deserves my devotion?

As I labored for the next year and a half with my brothers and sisters in the Living Room ministry, we continually honed our skills as "fishers of men," and in the midst of more than a few battles, we celebrated with great joy—while bringing in the sheaves! Please listen to this old hippy as he looks back: There is no greater joy in life than to be a soul-winner for our God! Believe me.

SEVEN

Heavy Oil

I ABSOLUTELY LOVED my adventures in the Haight-Ashbury. Even so, I missed my friends and family back home. I started taking one-month journeys down to Southern California to preach on the beaches. I could draw a crowd of people if I just opened my mouth. I open-air preached and led people to Christ at Newport pier, among other places. I also took advantage of the free speech zones in the universities, places like Orange Coast College and different campuses. I was so excited about my relationship with God and the doors that he was opening. I was young, bushy-tailed, and willingly captured by the love of our Savior.

Now, at that particular time God was getting ready to pour out his Spirit in a wonderful way. It was something along the order of Joel's prophecy: "Your sons and daughters will prophesy, your young men will see visions, your old men will dream dreams, Even on my servants, both men and women, I will pour out my Spirit in those days."[11]

I doubt if anyone in the sixties realized the significance of what was about to happen. Nevertheless, it was fast on the way. I was living in a cutting-edge Christian community in Northern California that was birthing a major move of God. How blessed I feel to have been in the midst of it.

On one of these early journeys to Southern California, by "accident" I found a storefront mission just a little south of Los Angeles in Huntington Beach. God had already raised up several other Christian communities, and each one was different. This one was part of a group called Teen Challenge, and the ministry operated very similarly to the way we operated our Living Room mission, except it was more entertainment oriented. They'd have singers come in and put on a show and things like that. People would come and listen, and then the Christians would individually witness for Christ. It was one of the first things that bloomed out of the Jesus movement.

The director of the mission immediately related to me because I had a mission in Haight-Ashbury and he had a mission in Orange County. His name was Bob. He was a streetwise ex-biker with a lot of charisma. Because we were both evangelists, we related to one another even more. Bob was an "on fire," in-your-face Christian, and I was a roaming evangelist with a purpose from the throne. I witnessed to everyone in my life, with the total idea that I would be a sweet-smelling savor unto salvation to some and an ugly stench unto death to others. I intentionally tried to impact every single person for Christ who came into my atmosphere—for blessing or judgment.

So it happened that during this season when I lived in a Christ-centered community up in Northern California, I was led to a Christian community hundreds of miles to the south that helped drug addicts and street people. They brought me to their ministry base and invited me to have dinner and to stay at Bob's place while I was preaching, even though my parents lived close by in Newport Beach. I was still in my late teens, excited about launching myself out into the world and not having to depend on my folks.

So one night everybody at the Huntington Beach community was getting ready for bed, and Bob got down on his knees. He began to speak in tongues, and then he opened one eye and looked over at me to see my reaction. I had *never* in my life heard anybody speak in tongues, well, at least the way he did. I really didn't know what speaking in tongues was all about. When I was saved as a little boy and around my grandmother's church, there were people who stood up in the meetings and shouted out with shrieking glossolalia—you know, the typical Pentecostal, fanatical, shrill utterances. It blew my mind and was a little bit frightening. But here was this ex-heroin addict, ex-biker turned mission director, leading in glossolalia. I was so fascinated that he was praying in another language.

"Do you know what I'm doing?" he asked me.

"No," I said.

He went on to explain that the Lord has different gifts for his children. Bob told me that he would take me to a church where I also could get "filled" with the Holy Spirit. The church was called Fullerton Foursquare. The pastor's name was Chuck Kruse, and he was a rockabilly Pentecostal.

When we arrived the next day, there was a visiting evangelist from Texas on the platform. I don't even remember the man's name, but I definitely remember everybody coming up and begging me to get saved. A couple of persistent women in Pastor Kruse's flock kept saying, "Oh, honey, come to the altar with me and find Christ."

I told them repeatedly that I was already a believer, but it didn't matter. Finally, I said, "Sister, lady, listen! Read my lips! **I am born again!**"

But they would not believe me. I want to emphasize that those people could not accept me—*because of my outward appearance*. I had shoulder-length hair, and I did not trim the edges of my beard. In addition to being a hippy, I had taken a Nazarite vow, which meant I could not cut my hair, trim my beard, or drink any wine or grape products. It's in the Old Testament.[12] So anyway, I had taken the vow at that particular time, and I remember all these different saints holding my hand and trying to drag me down to the altar.

They kept saying, "Get saved."

"But I am saved."

"No, you're not." They would not accept my confession, but I refused to go down to the altar, because I had already been born again. I had been born again at eight years old. Let me tell all you hardcore unbelievers who might read these words: When you finally get saved, get saved. Sincerely receive Christ and his free gift of grace and love. Establish the teaching of salvation in your life and don't doubt what God has provided for you, even when others don't receive you or believe you. But be warned that the toughest enemies you'll have will probably be some of the nearest ones. Your closest enemies will be your loved ones for a period of time.

So that sets the stage for this particular evening when a whole bunch of Pentecostals were coming up to me like piranhas. My very own brothers and sisters in the faith were *insisting* that I get saved, while I *insisted* that I was. But when there was a call to come forward to be filled with the Holy Spirit, that was a different story. That was why I had come there.

Like I said, I didn't realize what being filled with the Holy Spirit was all about, but I was open. I knew I already had the Holy Spirit, because I had conversations with the Lord. You know, there was a dialogue. He would talk to me, and I would talk to him. He would tell me to do things, to go places, and to say specific things. When I was obedient, it was like magic—wonderful and miraculous things would happen.

And yet Bob had explained some things out of the Book of Acts that stirred my curiosity. Perhaps there was something more. That such a powerfully sinful man found the strength and power to overcome lust, heroin, and womanizing—it really captured my attention. I was interested. Having my own unique, particular set of problems, I took my life to the altar once again.

The visiting evangelist had been preaching away the whole time. He was sweating like a pig. He was screaming, ranting and raving, and strutting around while whipping the microphone cord out in great loops across the stage. He would go back and forth like a hunter, pressing in for the bull's-eye. He was just carrying on, all the while with a white hanky in his hand. He was sweating profusely and continually wiping his face with the hanky. He seemed, you know, *unruly*, which was hard for a hippy non-conformist like myself to admit. I had never seen a Pentecostal preacher strut his stuff on the platform like that before.

When I finally walked forward, this man slapped his hand on my forehead and screamed, "Woo-hoo! Thank you, Jesus! Thank you, Jesus!" The volume was way over the top and way past acceptable. He was not only sweating, but he was sweating through his shirt, which was soaking wet. But when he laid his hands on my head, heaven came down! It wasn't a light, fluffy experience. It was heavy oil. The power of the Holy Spirit started coming down through him as an instrument of ministry, and the power of God filled my whole body with about ten thousand volts of electricity.

I said in my mind, "How can I even survive this? How am I going to live through this experience?"

God filled every atom of my being with the resurrection power of Jesus Christ. There was not one ounce of my body that wasn't filled with the power of the Holy Spirit.

And then I said, "Ohhh!" and "Ahhh!" It was beyond anything I had ever experienced.

I had always been the type of person who, when I thought that something was good, wanted to share the experience with everyone. Back when I was taking LSD and following Timothy Leary, I went out and bought a lot of LSD with my own money. It wasn't even illegal yet. I started turning on all my neighbors, brothers, and all my friends because I wanted people to experience LSD. I was even going to slip it in my parents' thermos bottle. Real zeal! I did give LSD to my brothers and friends, but thank God, I didn't actually give it to my parents. The bottom line is that I love to share a good thing. God wired me to want to give away a good thing as fast as I got it. Only in this case, the "it" was a person, the magnificent third person of the Trinity, our comforter, guide, and baptizer.

To me, most of life can be summed up by these Jim Croce lyrics: *"There never seems to be enough time to do the things you wanna do—once you find them."*[13] After my baptism, the Holy Spirit and I were off to the races, trying to reach as many people as possible with the time that I had. The power of God never rested on me like that before! After that initial experience in the church, I had many infillings of the Holy Spirit and my communication with Jesus became stronger. My witness for the Lord became bolder. I became unstoppable. I was driven by a need to tell people how much Jesus loved me, to tell others about our relationship together, and that they could have this love, power, and overcoming victory in their lives also. It's available to each of us. I led a lot of people to the Lord before I was baptized in the Holy Spirit, but after I was baptized, I was able to lead *hundreds* to Christ—so it is "not by might, nor by power, **but by the Spirit of the Lord!**"[14]

I'm persuaded in my theology that your relationship with God and Jesus hinges on the fountainhead of the Holy Spirit's work in your life as you walk in submission and obedience to his lordship and kingdom—Hallelujah! Let's have a few Holy Spirit breakdowns on this journey, where we just shout out, *"Unto him be glory in the church both now and evermore!"* and *"Unto the King eternal, immortal, invisible, the only wise God be honor and glory and power and dominion forever and ever!"* Then we can get caught up with the whole idea and revelation of what it means. Now *that's* a Holy Spirit breakdown! I'm having a good time even writing about this!

FIG NEWTONS IN BED

Let me interject a little amusing story that relates to this subject. Shortly after my experience at Pastor Kruse's church, I was visiting my parents. I was trying out my wings for speaking in tongues in my bedroom, or ex-bedroom. So I was having a prayer time in my room alone, speaking in my prayer language. I still hadn't fully discovered what tongues was all about. I just knew that speaking in tongues made me feel good and made me feel bold. So I was in my room secretly speaking in tongues when my mother happened to turn on the hose outside the bedroom window. As she was watering the front yard, she heard me.

She came into the house and burst into my room, yelling with her motherly dominion, "What are you doing? Are you speaking in tongues in this house? I heard you speak in tongues!"

I said, "Mom, I believe in glossolalia. I'm not speaking in tongues—I'm practicing glossolalia!"

She said, "Ohhhh," and then turned around and left my room.

It was like that TV commercial where the mom says, "Are you eating cookies in bed?" And the kid says, "I'm not eating cookies. I'm eating Fig Newtons!"

And so I told my mom no and denied speaking in tongues. I denied it because she was screaming and yelling and carrying on, telling me I couldn't do it. She had a bad experience in a Pentecostal church one time and wanted nothing to do with any of it. I threw her a curveball and told her I was practicing glossolalia, which is a fancy word for "tongue-talking."

Anyway, my newfound gift of the infilling of the Holy Spirit changed the course of my life and the direction of my ministry.

Suddenly, when I would begin to speak about Jesus, the atmosphere would fill with his reality. The presence of the Shekinah glory of God would accompany my words. I have to say that my ability to preach, understand the Word of God, and witness for Christ became multiplied when I got filled with his power: "But ye shall receive power, after that the Holy Ghost is come upon you: and ye shall be witnesses unto me both in Jerusalem, Judea, Samaria, and to the uttermost parts of the earth."[15]

MY LOVELY BRIDE

On one of my many trips back home, I returned to the place of my visitation and calling. I love Tahquitz Canyon. I hiked up the familiar winding trail surrounded by all the trees and rocks that lined the crystal-clear, bubbling stream. There were occasional waterfalls too. Eventually, I came upon a large pond area with several huge rocks. On one of the boulders I saw a beautiful young girl lying out in the warm sunshine. She was completely nude, which was normal for the Canyon. I had my Bible and walked over to her. I felt the presence of God as she opened her eyes.

She was a runaway and had just dropped some acid. I knew this girl and had witnessed to her before. She came from a very broken home. I gently started talking to her about the Lord. She was stoned, and I didn't want to blow her trip. I sat next to her, opened my Bible, and started reading to her. Soon there were tears flowing down her pretty cheeks. I asked if she wanted to receive Jesus in her heart, and through the tears, she said, "Yes."

She prayed with me, and it was absolutely glorious. I asked if she wanted to be baptized, and again she said, "Yes," without hesitation. Just as she was, she walked with me into the pool of water, and I baptized her in the name of the Father, the Son, and of the mighty Holy Spirit. As she went under the waters of baptism (representing the death of our old nature) and came up into the light (representing resurrection and a new life), she glowed.

The drugs were completely overpowered by the manifest presence of God, and Connie Bremer became a child of the King. She immediately put her dress on, and I joyously brought her to our communal ranch way up north in Novato. Several months later in April 1968, she became my lovely bride.

Back in the late sixties, God was setting the stage for a remarkable revival. It was an ingathering of souls. It was a move of the Holy Spirit. It was a wave in a set of waves and a signpost of the impending return of Christ. There is another huge wave approaching, an end-time harvest that is bigger than you can imagine, when God is going to pour out his Spirit like never before. "'In the last days,' God says, 'I will pour out my spirit on all people. Your sons and daughters will prophesy, your young men will see visions, your old men will dream dreams. Even on my servants, both men and women, I will pour out my Spirit in those days.'"[16]

I am instructed to tell you that Jesus is coming back—soon!

Lonnie and Connie

64

EIGHT

The Jesus People

SO THERE WERE five families that lived together for two years in Novato, laboring for the Lord in the Haight-Ashbury. My wife, Connie, loved living in the House of Acts. There was *never* a dull moment. However, we were the first family to leave, and that was because every month I was hitchhiking down the coast of California as a vessel of the Lord, and this eventually resulted in a big change. People would pick me up hitching, and I'd witness about Christ. Like I said, I had a **passion** for witnessing. I was driven to share Christ because he was *so* good to me. I had this living, vital relationship with the Son of God and was absolutely compelled to tell people about the Lord. It was my reason for living! Serving the Lord twenty-four hours a day, seven days a week—and I was *very* fulfilled with my work.

I had so many experiences hitchhiking. It was like the Lord had a special plan to hook me up with the right people. I would pray for divine appointments, and boy, would I get them—lonely people, happy people, curious people, angry people, loaded people, hurting people, and seeking people, along with every kind of drama and situation imaginable. It would all present itself, and then the Lord would blow my mind by giving me wisdom and supernatural words of knowledge and love for the people. It's such a gigantic lie from the "dark side" that serving God is boring or that being a truly "born from above" believer is giving up all the good stuff. I was energized. Jesus said, "I came to give you life, that you may have it abundantly!"[17]

I would hitchhike all the way down to Southern California to witness to my family, to people I went to school with, and really, to anyone. I had been very popular because of the TV show, and as a result, I was able to lead many people to Christ. I'd go to the Orange County Fair, get out in the middle of the open area, and yell,

"Hey!!" I'd jump up and down—I really looked like a freak. I could draw hundreds of people like that and always felt the anointing of God fall on me when I stepped out in boldness. I'd preach and give an altar call before the police got there! Sometimes I'd go down to the Newport pier dressed like a hippy and yell again, "Hey!!" I'd jump up and down with my hair flying in the wind. Everybody would gather around the crazy man. Then I'd preach the gospel! God would put something on it. I'd give an altar call, and fifty people in bathing suits and bikinis would accept the Lord. It was really wonderful.

So one day when I was visiting Southern California, a young, clean-cut, short-haired man picked me up hitchhiking. Pretty soon he started sharing Christ with me and, I guess, was trying to lead me to the Lord.

I told him, "Hey, partner, you pick up hitchhikers and witness to them. I hitch to share Christ with people who pick me up. I'm already saved, redeemed, washed in the blood!"

It took a little while to convince him that I was truly born again, because he had never met a hippy Christian. I pulled out my sword—the living Word of God—and we discussed things of the kingdom.

Finally, he said, "I want you to meet some people. Would that be okay? They have been wanting to meet a real hippy. You will blow their minds!"

I was game.

We drove to this middle-class Orange County neighborhood, and he knocked on the door of one of the houses. It turned out that my new friend, John Nicholson, was dating the daughter of a local pastor. After a minute or so, Pastor Chuck Smith answered the door, and I would venture to say that a divine appointment of heavenly significance manifested itself into the affairs of men. That might sound a little grandiose, but within a very short time, thousands and thousands of precious souls were added to the kingdom of God and a major move of the Spirit swept up the coast of California and around the world. It was definitely a God thing.

I can't remember the exact words that we spoke in our introduction, but a book named *The Reproducers*, published a year or two later, reports our first meeting like this:

John and Lonnie knocked on the Smiths' door later that evening. What the Smiths saw and felt almost did blow their minds! Not because they couldn't equate Christians with beards and long hair. But because they saw in this almost frail young man an unusual character and capacity to love. "This might be the very person to help us begin reaching the great numbers of hippies who are migrating to the beach areas," mused Chuck.

As the evening progressed Chuck shared his dream with Lonnie and John. "If you could help John and a few of us share Christ with the hippies on the beach," said Chuck, "I believe they would respond. You speak their language and you know better than any of us how, what and why they think and feel the way they do. Furthermore you could stay with us for a couple of weeks and help me understand what makes them tick."

"I like the idea," said Lonnie, "but I am married and live in San Francisco."

"No problem," said Chuck. "Bring your wife. She can stay too."

In a couple of weeks Lonnie and his wife, Connie, returned and moved in with the Smiths. Several days later two other hippies that Lonnie led to the Lord moved in, and in the true spirit of having all things in common, began to share and help themselves to each others belongings. Connie frequently popped into Jan's closet and borrowed clothes just as if they were her own. But no one in the Smith family resented this. "We were fascinated with their genuine openness and reality," said Kay. "There was so much natural beauty and love bubbling forth we couldn't resist them." And before Lonnie and Connie returned to San Francisco neither could the people at Calvary.[18]

When Connie and I returned to Novato, I was very excited about our time in Southern California. Connie had enjoyed Chuck and Kay Smith and the small Calvary Chapel congregation, but she was not ready to make any major changes in our lives. She loved living at our House of Acts commune in Novato, and so did I. However, a phone call and an invitation from Chuck Smith to join the staff at Calvary Chapel followed shortly.

In a big fight Connie told me, "I'll make you sorry for the rest of your life if you force me to leave the ranch." Sadly, that's pretty much how it turned out in the long run. I was absolutely positive that God had called us back to Southern California, and I know for sure he did. Nevertheless, I failed miserably at communicating with Connie and at meeting her needs. Like so many do in marriage, I charged forward time after time, making my bride feel perpetually in second place. Like they say, "Hindsight is twenty-twenty." But I do want to mention that I adored Connie and always will. In the end, I pulled rank, and we closed a huge chapter of our lives in Northern California. Our time in the Haight-Ashbury was over. We headed south.

A TIDAL WAVE

To tell all the stories that unfolded over the next few years would be almost impossible. It's like what it says at the end of the Gospel of John: "And there are also many other things which Jesus did, the which, if they should be written every one, I suppose that even the world itself could not contain the books that should be written."[19]

Still, I'll try to hit some of the highlights from my perspective of what soon became widely known as the Jesus People movement. Hopefully, the Lord will allow me to give you a glimpse of the revival and a touch of the glorious anointing that he poured out on our generation. It was birthed in the Haight-Ashbury, but it hit the beaches of Southern California like a spiritual tidal wave.

When we first arrived in Costa Mesa, the Calvary Chapel congregation, which was about eighty people on a good Sunday, had rented a small house that Chuck named the House of Miracles. He wanted to model it after our House of Acts up north. Several of us immediately converged on the beaches, and we led dozens and dozens of young people to the Lord right away. I would pray with them, then bring them home. The house only had two bedrooms, but pretty soon we had people sleeping all over the place. It was crazy! People were on the couch, in the hallway, in the garage, camping out in the backyard, everywhere. A young elder from the church, John Higgins, oversaw the budding commune along with Connie and me. John was a good organizer and totally "on fire."

Eventually, we had a tiny bit of order happening. We held regular Bible studies in the home and took our new spiritual babes to church and other events. We also took new believers with us back to the beaches and to the streets so they could tell their friends about a loving God who rescued us. It was like magic.

Mod Church In CM Delivers Youths From Dangers

The young people became the evangelists. The church began to grow by leaps and bounds, packed wall-to-wall with long-haired hippies—beards, beads, bare feet, and all—on Sunday mornings. It upset some of the old fogies in the congregation. However, most of them got over it when they saw the Lord moving so powerfully with us.

We opened several other homes, including a converted motel in Riverside, in a short period of time. I lost count of how many Christian communes sprang up during the Jesus People movement, but I'm told it was over a hundred. We would go back to Tahquitz Canyon and everywhere else to share Christ. The Lord was bringing in a lost generation by the droves. I never claimed to be the only evangelist of this move of God. It was more like Tom Sawyer putting the other kids to work on the fence—the new converts did the legwork.

Here's a little side note: I have been accused of being a rebel, which is partially true, but the fact is that *every* time the Lord has used me, it has always been in a team situation. We need each other. We don't need a bunch of Lone Rangers. It goes for ministries also. God raised up many other ministries besides ours during this special time on the West Coast, but Calvary Chapel definitely was the epicenter. It's documented history.

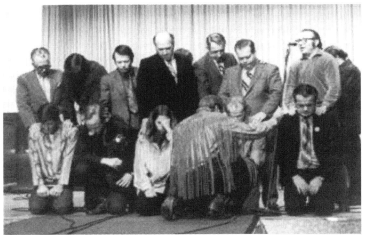

Lonnie being ordained by Chuck Smith at Calvary Chapel

JIMMY KEMPNER

At the House of Miracles, or maybe it was at the Bluetop Motel, I was awakened out of a dead sleep at two o'clock in the morning by all kinds of commotion. Let me first describe how I looked. Here's a snapshot: I was dressed in an old-fashioned cotton flannel nightgown that went down to my ankles; I had shoulder-length hair, a long beard, and a white cotton flannel nightcap with a ball on the end of it. Anyway, I was disturbed from my sleep by all the noise coming from some guy freaking out right in front of our place. Let me remind you that this was a Christian community where we had families and babies, and this dude was just literally raising hell.

I came out my front door and looked down the alley. I immediately recognized the wild, young cowboy who was waving his arms around, yelling, and slurring out profanity. It was Jimmy Kempner. He was lifting up the name of God in complete disrespect, being an absolute blasphemer. Jimmy Kempner was high on LSD. Now, I had gone to high school with Jimmy. We had hung out at the teen dances at the fairgrounds and other places. I knew him pretty well, but I never saw him *this* wasted. He knew that I was now a Jesus freak, and he was saying everything that he thought was clever. Over and over he blasphemed the name of Jesus.

I took authority over that demonic demonstration in Jesus' name, and we led Jimmy to salvation that night. He was set free. The One he was cursing saved him. Jesus willingly became a curse and allowed Roman nails to be pounded through his hands and feet so that he could save Jimmy Kempner.

Jimmy was one of my converts who quickly grew in the Lord and preached the gospel himself in a significant way. God put an anointing on his words, and he preached to huge crowds at Knott's Berry Farm and even at Disneyland. Because of our contacts in the corporation of Disneyland, they started to have "Christian Night," when Andre Crouch and Jimmy Kempner would pack out the "happiest place on Earth." In fact, Jimmy was the first evangelist to preach at Disneyland, and he went on to labor in the ministry and make me proud of his usefulness to God.

Sometimes God seems to put everything in a single period of time, a time when God will use somebody, raise them up, and then pull them down. He has just as much permission to pull you down as he has permission to lift you up. The Lord always impressed on me this rhema: "Promotion cometh neither from the east, nor from the west, nor from the south. But God is the judge: he putteth down one, and setteth up another."[20] As his children, we have a big part to play in who he raises up and who he scourges. It's no fun to receive the discipline of the Lord. Believe me, I know something of this. At the same time, be encouraged, brothers and sisters, that no matter how severe his rod might seem, God will never leave us nor forsake his children. He disciplines us out of love for our own good. Remember, "Man looks at the outward appearance, but God looks at the heart." Stay close, Jimmy!

WEDNESDAY NIGHT

Things were happening so fast that it was hard to wrap our minds and emotions around all of the changes. One thing was for certain: It was exciting. We never knew what was next. God was blessing our efforts to serve him morning, noon, and night. We were leading hundreds of hippies and young people to the Lord on the beaches, in our communities, in church, in Bible studies, in restaurants, at concerts, and just about everywhere. The electrifying atmosphere is so hard to capture into words. It was tangible. Everyone's faith level soared. Some of the parents were coming to Christ when they saw the change in their kids, when they saw them getting off drugs, getting healed, and being delivered from all kinds of things. It was precious.

Our church was growing so quickly that soon there were

hundreds and hundreds attending. In no time at all, there were over a thousand people at each of our meetings. Chuck went to two services on Sunday morning and eventually to three. We started baptizing new believers in the ocean, and the baptisms themselves began to explode with the Spirit of God touching everyone.

People were getting saved as they came to watch others get baptized, and then, minutes later, they were baptized themselves right on the beach at Corona del Mar.

We outgrew our church building a couple of times, and God started giving us new songs from sincere, talented young believers. Contemporary Christian music was birthed in our midst. Almost overnight there were bands and musicians like Children of the Day, Love Song, Larry Norman, Barry McGuire, Andrae Crouch and the Disciples, Keith Green, 2nd Chapter of Acts, and on and on. There was an anointing in the air that seemed to cover everything we touched.

ONE WAY!

We were and are the Jesus People. Our peace symbol is not an upside-down, broken cross. It is a dove descending upon the Prince of Peace. It is the secret Ichthus fish symbol used by Christians two thousand years ago to avoid persecution by Rome. But our ultimate peace symbol is an upright, empty cross because Christ conquered death for all mankind—and he is risen! Our sign to each other and to the world is the "One Way!" sign, which is the index finger raised

in victory, representing that there is only one way to God! Jesus declared, "I am the way, the truth, and the life. No one comes to the Father except through me! I am the good shepherd, and I willingly gave up my life so that you might live."[21]

Chuck Smith was our loving pastor and Bible teacher. Many of us nicknamed him "Papa Chuck." He is not only a good teacher, he is a *great* teacher. I hung on to his every sentence. He confirmed almost everything line by line that the Holy Spirit had been teaching and revealing to me. He instructed me in the Word of God, for which I am forever grateful. He was instantly the hippies' father figure, and you know my history with father figures. I desperately needed a good and godly role model. We all do.

I had just turned twenty years old and was officially assigned the role as evangelist and Calvary Chapel youth pastor. It opened up so many more doors than just "hitchhiking for Jesus." I was praising God night and day. I was full of energy and motivation and was just like Jesus in that I didn't want anyone to be lost. I wanted everyone to get saved and enter into eternal life in a perfect kingdom. We are definitely not in a perfect situation right now, but there is one coming! The Holy Spirit continued to give me revelation, divine guidance, confirmations, impartations, and love, love, love.

Lonnie and Chuck Smith ministering at Calvary Chapel

Pretty soon I was given every Wednesday night to minister to the people. How seriously I took that responsibility! I sought God with all my heart before each meeting. In my desire to serve God, I learned early on in my Christian experience that if the anointing was there, it was glorious, but if it lifted off for whatever reason, it was no fun at all. We need to pay attention, we need to obey, we need to keep our hearts right with God. Believe me, I failed many times in every department—but I tried. When I would fail, God would pick me up and instruct me with this truth: We fail our way into the kingdom of God. It starts with grace, and it ends with grace. Like the Word says, grace is not an excuse to fail or to sin.[22] It is there to cover us, put our feet back on the straight and narrow, and mold us into sons and daughters. He is looking for availability and a teachable, sincere heart. Remember, it's "not by might, nor by power, but by my Spirit, saith the Lord!"

The Wednesday night meetings were glorious. His presence and anointing was on every single meeting. Hundreds and then thousands came out to a midweek church service in Orange County. Think about that for a minute. It was not Christmas or Easter, but the middle of a workweek. Every seat was filled, the aisles were full, the front was packed with kids sitting on the floor, outside was packed with people listening on speakers and looking in the windows. I would share and preach, and maybe Marsha Carter would sing "Come to the Water." She wrote the lyrics in minutes one day. The Lord just downloaded it very supernaturally. It became our signature song for the revival. It was and is the Jesus People tribute to our King and was famous around the world. Marsha would sing like an angel of God:

"Jesus, I give you my heart and my soul;
I know that without God, I'd never be whole.
Savior, you opened all the right doors,
And I thank you and praise you from Earth's humble shores;
Take me, I'm yours.

And Jesus said, 'Come to the water,
Stand by my side.
I know you are thirsty, you won't be denied.
I felt every teardrop when in darkness you cried,
And I strove to remind you
That for those tears I died."

After I would preach, I'd give an altar call. I could feel the Lord drawing people with his presence. In a sense, it was effortless, but at the same time, it required a focus on our part. I learned so much about the Holy Spirit during those Wednesday night services. It is all about being "in tune" with him. Jesus said he would make us fishers of men, and his presence is the bait. I mean, week after week, when the invitation went out, the altar was *filled* with thirsty souls.

Hundreds and hundreds of decisions were made with tears, repentance, laughter, and joy beyond words.

At one point in a two-year stretch, we were baptizing an estimated five hundred people every month, with a crowd of thousands watching and cheering and crying on the beach. It was my vision from Tahquitz Canyon being fulfilled before my very eyes. I absolutely loved every single second, and I praise God to whom I give all the glory!

PERSONAL AND SPECIAL

I'd like to share about one particular Wednesday night at Calvary Chapel. It's very personal and special to me. I was, by this point, twenty-one years old, and we were in full revival. The huge baptisms each month had caught the attention of the news media. I was interviewed multiple times, quoted in articles, filmed, recorded, put on the radio, and on and on. I think my live TV experience as a teenager on the Casey Kasem show helped me handle the bright lights and attention. I knew that if Hollywood could do it, the Lord could do it better.

Nevertheless, it is hard to stay humble, especially if you have a damaged image of yourself and need approval (like I did). So on the one hand, you can realize that the Lord has allowed you to become a reigning prince, while on the other hand, you know that he can burst your bubble real quick if you allow your human pride to deceive you.

Anyway, at this particular Wednesday night service, we had *Time* magazine, a BBC news team, and KQED 9 Public TV from the Bay Area, which later produced a documentary about the revival. They were all in the meeting at the same time. So there I was, twenty-one years old, standing up in front of at least a thousand people, preaching the gospel. That's the setting.

By the way, *Time* did a major story on June 21, 1971, with an article titled "The New Rebel Cry: Jesus is Coming!" The cover of the magazine had a cool illustration of Jesus surrounded by the words: "The Jesus Revolution." The article covered Calvary Chapel and the massive baptisms at Corona del Mar. I'm told that the artist who designed the cover also designed some of the Beatles' album covers, but I'm not sure if that's the case. I love that magazine cover and piece of artwork.

So back to the service that night. My mother lived down the block from the church, but my stepfather wouldn't walk across the street to hear me preach for nothing. My stepdad raised me in 100 percent, unadulterated rejection. There wasn't anything he ever acted out toward me that wasn't from a place of rejection. Plenty of pain. Believe me, he let me know over and over that I was a nutcase, had always been a nutcase, and was now some kind of fanatical Jesus freak. However, one of my brothers had run away from home. That is, one of my half brothers, one of Lyle's "real" sons, had run away and was having problems with drugs. So my stepfather said, "Let's go drive to the church and see if he is there."

When they got to the church and saw how packed out the parking lot was with people everywhere, my stepdad turned to my mom and asked, "Why in the world would *anybody* want to come and hear Lonnie?"

Well, my dad turned around and went home, but my mother snuck into our service. She had never heard me speak or been to anything that I was involved with. She was way in the back of the crowd, so far back that I couldn't recognize her. Besides, I would get so caught up in the Spirit when I was ministering that I was not really looking at the people. I was looking at what the Spirit of God was doing. That was my focus.

My mother told me what happened next for her. I heard her tell it twice. She explained that while I was preaching on the stage, she said to herself, "Where did Lonnie learn all of these things? When?"

Later as I was giving the altar call, I had this *strong* impression come upon me. As a result, I gave one of the longest altar calls I had ever given at Calvary Chapel. I kept saying, "There's somebody out there who needs to come to the Lord." Then I got quiet and waited. The church was silent. A minute seemed like an hour. I repeated it several times, and we would again wait quite a while even though the front of the church was filled with people who had come forward. I still felt led to wait some more.

"There is somebody out there who—I am getting in my spirit— needs to come to the Lord. You need to surrender your life to the Lord, and you're not doing it, and you have to—**now!**" I remember. I said it just like that.

Then I heard this loud sobbing coming from the back of the church. I looked up, and my mother was running down the aisle to the altar. The only problem was that the church was completely packed out with people everywhere. There were as many people outside as there were inside. She was literally stepping on people because the aisle was so full.

She explained to me later like this: "As you were saying that somebody had to come forward, I looked up, and you turned into a white light. All I could see on the platform where you were standing was a ball of white light with three rainbows coming out of it! The rainbows were just going out of the light, and I said, 'That's not my son! That's not Lonnie!'"

My mom knew at that moment that Jesus Christ was really inside of me. When she saw the ball of white light where I was standing, with the rainbows permeating out of the light, she felt an electrifying power like white heat drop down through the top of her head and flow through her whole body, lifting her out of her chair. It was *that* power that brought her forward.

She told me, "I don't remember even one foot touching the ground!"

My mother received Jesus that night, as did many other hungry and hurting hearts who responded to the call and came forward to the altar of God.

As Jesus says,

"Come to the water,
Stand by my side.
I know you are thirsty, you won't be denied.
I felt every teardrop when in darkness you cried,
And I strove to remind you
That for those tears I died."

That very same resurrection power of Jesus that my mother experienced is available to each of us—every day of the week!

NINE

Daughter of Destiny

AS GOD'S LOVE was poured out on Southern California, it more and more continued to catch the attention of the entire world. Thousands and thousands of young people were coming to Christ. It became commonplace to see TV cameras, reporters, and other media people in our meetings at Calvary Chapel. Cameras were everywhere at the huge ocean baptisms at Corona del Mar. Chuck Smith was the fatherly pastor and Bible teacher. I was the hippy evangelist. Our pictures were plastered all over the place in newspapers and then in major stories in *Time* magazine, *Look*, and many other mainstream outlets.

Film documentaries were produced, my favorite being *Jesus People* by Pyramid Films. They featured one of my messages and altar calls at our packed-out church. This was even before we outgrew the future Maranatha Village building and moved into the giant tent. Pyramid Films did a wonderful job capturing a touch of the Holy Spirit's presence in one of the Corona del Mar ocean baptisms. You can feel the anointing and see the powerful impact on people with your own eyes. Media at its best! The revival was absolutely glorious!

For about seven years, I would go up to the Shrine Auditorium in Los Angeles each month to the Kathryn Kuhlman meetings. I witnessed undeniable miracles. The presence of the Holy Spirit would be so powerful that it overwhelmed me. I was drawn to those meetings like a magnet and longed for the gift of healing and miracles in

Kathryn Kuhlman

my own life. I bombarded heaven with my petitions. There were so many people getting healed in Kathryn Kuhlman's meetings that buses would be lined up in the parking lot from all over the United States and, really, the world. There were people flying in from South America and everywhere.

Before each meeting started, it felt like feeding time at the LA Zoo. Thousands were lined up before the doors even opened. People were pushing wheelchairs around, rushing to get near the stage. There was excitement and anticipation in the air. I loved every minute and couldn't get enough. Little did I know that God would answer my heart's desire and there would come a day when I would be ministering alongside Kathryn Kuhlman at places like the Hollywood Palladium. There would also come a day when I would witness blind eyes open beneath my hands. This unusual and unique woman taught me about the Holy Spirit, and she is my absolute hero of the faith.

One week in 1971 in the midst of the revival, we took several busloads of our young, "on fire" Jesus People to Kathryn Kuhlman's TV set in Hollywood. She had personally invited Chuck Smith and Duane Pederson, along with hundreds of our young converts, to be featured and interviewed on her popular weekly TV show, *I Believe in Miracles.* I think we filmed eight programs all together. Recently, a friend was able to get copies of four of the thirty-minute programs. Somehow in the hustle and bustle of the day, I missed seeing the broadcasts. I actually saw them for the first time exactly twenty years after they originally aired on TV. What a tremendous joy that was for me! We all looked so young—and we were. My friend Tom Stipe looked like a baby.

Anyway, one of the reasons these films are so special to me is because they captured the first time I met Kathryn Kuhlman. I had attended lots of her meetings but had never personally met her. However, on that day, she asked for me. On national television she cupped my face in her anointed hands and blessed me!

Let me describe that day at the CBS studio in a little more detail. There was a huge crowd of us surrounding Kathryn Kuhlman on the set. The entire studio was packed out with new converts. The program opened with the theme song "He Touched Me." Our young Jesus People all raised their hands with the "One Way!" sign at the song's conclusion.

Kathryn Kuhlman joined in with her raised hand, announcing that she was also one of us, a "born-from-above Jesus person." I was sitting on the floor close to her among the shoulder-to-shoulder crowd. We were fanned out completely around her. Hundreds more filled every seat in the theater-style set. It was electric to be there! The sixty-two-year-old Miss Kuhlman was introducing Duane Pederson and Chuck Smith, but then she turned to me and said, "Are you Lonnie?"

"Yes."

She said, "I thought so. And Chuck, you don't know this, but Lonnie called me up the other morning and said, 'Kathryn Kuhlman, I'm Lonnie.' He began talking with

me, and when he referred to you, he referred to you as 'Daddy Chuck.' You didn't realize it, Lonnie, but that's the greatest compliment you could have paid to your pastor. Maybe you better just call me 'Mama Kathryn.'"

The whole crowd laughed along with her raspy, hearty laugh, but the truth is Kathryn Kuhlman was definitely a wonderful spiritual mother and mentor to me. She had such a huge impact on my life. Before she died in 1976, she laid hands on me in a prayer of impartation. I obviously believe in women in ministry according to their calling.

In fact, I believe that the anointing that is resting on my life can be traced directly to another woman of God—Aimee Semple McPherson—because of her influence on both Kathryn Kuhlman and Chuck Smith. Chuck came out of the Foursquare Church founded by Aimee, and Aimee, who died in 1944, definitely influenced Kathryn Kuhlman. They have many indirect links, and people constantly compared Miss Kuhlman to her famous female healing predecessor. Chuck Smith taught me in the Word. Kathryn Kuhlman taught me in the Holy Ghost.

AIMEE

Speaking of Aimee Semple McPherson, her private and personal secretary of many years began to attend Calvary Chapel. By that time, the secretary was a quite elderly lady in her eighties, and I asked her to share about Aimee. She always called Aimee "Sister." She began explaining that Aimee came back from years in China because her husband had died on the mission field and she was left a widow. One day back in the thirties or thereabout, Aimee was lecturing in LA about divine healing, and there was a crippled man in a wheelchair in the audience.

Aimee's secretary told me, "The crippled man challenged Aimee. He yelled out from the audience, *'What can your God do for me?'* So Sister left the platform and went behind the stage. She went down some steps, got on her knees, and prayed: 'This man is challenging me, O Lord. What do I do? O God, Jesus, tell me what to do!'"

And that was the simplicity and the secret of Aimee's ministry. She said, as a widow with no husband to lean on, "Lord, what should I do?" Aimee was leaning into Jesus Christ as a husband, asking, "Lord, what's your counsel? What should I do? He's challenging the word that I'm preaching."

Then the Holy Spirit spoke to Aimee in that still, small voice. He said, "You go up on the platform, stretch your hand out to the man, and say, '**Be thou whole in the name of Jesus!**'"

Aimee obeyed, and after she spoke those words, the man stood up with his bones popping so loudly that the whole audience could hear. He stood up over six feet tall with his bones popping and snapping back in place. He went from being a twisted wreck of a cripple to standing on his feet, handsome and whole and instantaneously healed! That was the miracle that shot Aimee into national notoriety. Work miracles, and they will beat a path to your door!

I said to her secretary, "Tell me some more. Tell me about the most beautiful healing that you can remember in Aimee's ministry."

"Well, Sister was in her high form. And Charlie Chaplin was sitting over to her right, and Gloria Swanson was sitting over here, and the platform was full of flowers. There was a thirteen-year-old boy born blind who was instantly healed in the meeting while Aimee was preaching. He said, 'Oh look, Mother, the beautiful woman!'"

When Aimee realized that the boy had been healed, she had him touch his finger to her nose, and then she joyously jumped around. She used to play things up like that. I believe you'll never be involved in working public miracles unless you can be somewhat of a performer. You know, you have to have a "go for it" attitude to pray for people's eyes or for crippled legs. You usually start with something easy like a cold or the flu.

My first miracle was for warts. Maybe you get a little chuckle out of that. The laugh scale usually peaks at about a two. It does that whenever I tell this story, because wart healings are probably on a scale of a two. You want to know the difference between God healing a wart and God healing a tumor? No difference. It's the same healing power. Wart healings are on a two, but it is the same power when God heals a cancerous tumor, which most people would consider a ten.

One day I was praying in my room before my Wednesday night meeting at Calvary, and the Lord said, "Lonnie, I'm going to heal people in the meeting tonight."

Oh boy, I got excited! And then I heard a different voice say, "Yeah, but what if he doesn't?"

We all know that voice. It's the devil. He always comes in like that.

I thought to myself, "Yeah, what if he doesn't!"

Then you know what? That good feeling left me all day. I had to suffer in doubt and fear. It was just like when the Lord said to Peter in the boat, "Hey, you were doing so well! What happened out there?"

The disciples had been shocked to see Jesus walking on the water. They thought they were seeing a ghost or something off in the distance.

Peter was mouthy. "Hey, if that's you, bid me to come unto you!"

"Come," Jesus said.

Peter jumped out of the boat and walked on the sea toward Jesus. He did it. He walked on water, but when he noticed the waves around him and took his eyes off Jesus, he started to sink. That's what happens to all of us—"Help! I'm perishing!"

We all know that Jesus rescued him, but many don't realize that in the process, Peter got to walk on water *twice!* There is much to be said about a go-getter attitude. Let me remind you again, it can be truthfully said, "We fail our way into the kingdom." Jesus lovingly and powerfully pulls us out of the water and gets us going again.

So that night at Calvary Chapel, I got up on the platform to preach. I announced to the crowd, "God has a special treat. He is going to heal people tonight!"

Instead of people's eyes lighting up, people started falling asleep. It was like the guy who, slumping down in his chair at church, finally wakes up when it's over and asks, "Was he good, honey?"

I said, "Okay," and I called out a cold healing. Everyone started hacking and coughing.

I said to myself, "This isn't fun! This is *not* fuuuun!" I called out a wart healing, and everybody roared with laughter. It was not a two on the laughter scale that night by far. It was off the scale. I started sweating. I started sweating bullets, really. Finally, the meeting ended, and I was left going, "But I thought the Lord wanted to heal people."

Then this nineteen-year-old girl came up to me, holding in her hand a mass of warts that had separated themselves from the bottom of her foot in her shoe. Warts had taken over the bottom of her foot, and they came off in her shoe! Her foot was like a baby's bottom, it was so soft and smooth. I held the warts in my hand, amazed and thrilled—until I remembered that I had dismissed the meeting and people were walking out the door. No one got to see my miracle!

"Hey, wait! The meeting's not over! I got the warts!"

But it was too late. Almost everyone was out the door. I can tell you right now that most of us are not interested in working miracles unless people can see the performance. I was a victim of this. My need for approval, my thorn in the flesh.

God might say, "Go work miracles in your closet," and you're not going to want to do it. But that's what being an intercessor is all about. An intercessor is working miracles in a closet. Later in my life God revealed to me that the highest calling in the body of Christ is to intercede for the nations. How many faithful sons and daughters are fulfilling that call? Well, they are out there, thank God, and we need more intercessors as the days get darker and time gets shorter and shorter.

Now back to the CBS studio with Kathryn Kuhlman in 1971. It was so cool. Chuck Girard and Love Song sang their famous "Welcome Back." It sounded better than the album. People shared testimonies, and Kathryn Kuhlman interviewed Chuck Smith and many others. Marsha Carter and Children of the Day sang our theme song, "Come to the Water." It was captivating. It was "Holy Spirit goose bumps" all the way. Marsha sang and shared how the Lord gave her that song in a matter of minutes—ordinary people used in extraordinary ways. After her song, everyone in the studio raised the "One Way!" salute, and there was a precious moment of silence.

Then Duane Pederson said, "One of the young men, Kathryn, who has been so used of God is Lonnie Frisbee. And I wonder if Lonnie could just share with us now."

I stood up on national TV without any script and opened my mouth: "Well, the people tell me that I'm trying to look like Jesus. I can't think of anyone else I'd rather look like. Jesus—he changed my life, and I kinda relate to David the psalmist when he says that 'Thou has lifted me up from the dunghill and placed my feet on a solid rock.'[23] And Jesus has lifted me up out of a horrible pit, and he's washed my heart from all the sins and all the evil that I had gotten myself into, and since that, I'm all cleaned up now…and—"

Kathryn chimed in, "Isn't that a wonderful feeling?"

"Yeah!"

The whole audience laughed.

Kathryn added, "And only Jesus could have done it!"

"That's right. He's given me a message in my heart, and that's a message where he says, 'Go ye into all the world and preach the gospel.' He says that 'he that believes and is baptized shall be saved, and he that believes not, shall be damned,' and he said in his Word to me, I would receive power, after that the Holy Ghost would come upon me, and I waited upon the Lord, and the Holy Ghost came upon me all right![24] Yeah, I got it down to the tips of my toes!

"And so the message is that these are the last days and that Jesus Christ is returning really soon. And the prophet Joel and the prophet Peter said that in the last days God would pour out his Spirit upon all flesh and that his sons and daughters would prophesy, and that his servants and handmaidens would speak forth the anointed word of God.[25] I'm a servant of God, and I'm a child of God, and God is raising up from the very bottom—he's raising up the foolish and what the world considers dumb, and he's putting his Spirit upon them and anointing them, and they're starting to preach the gospel. And thousands of people are starting to get saved everywhere, and so—"

"It's thrilling!" Miss Kuhlman interrupted.

The audience laughed again.

Lonnie speaking on *I Believe in Miracles*

I continued, "And so, because these are the last days, God has chosen himself some prophets, and the church for so long has been expecting a certain mold of what a Christian should look like or what a Christian should be or what a Christian should say, and God is blowing everybody's minds. Because he's saving the hippies," (I put my hand on top of my head)—"and nobody thought a hippy could be saved!"

More laughter broke out. I absolutely love it when people laugh. It's a good sign. God opens people up with laughter—and then stabs them with divine truth!

"And so he's pulled us up, given us the message, and we're going forth proclaiming the good news: 'Jesus is coming back, repent, and turn to the Lord. Save yourselves from this evil generation because he comes to judge the quick and the dead.'"[26]

"How has he changed your life, Lonnie?"

"Well, the Lord says, 'If any man be in Christ, he is a new creature. Old things pass away, and behold all things become new.'[27] He's changed me all around."

"Really?"

"Inside out. Through and through," I answered.

"And the things you once loved, you have no desire for at all, right?"

"Just went right out. He says, 'I'll take your stony heart of unbelief, and I'll put a new heart within you and place my Spirit within you too.' And so everything changes. He says, 'I'll become a well of living water gushing forth from within you,' and that well of living water gets out everything else."[28]

Because of my future failures, my critics will jump on this confession of faith that I made at twenty-two years of age, but I want to mention that it is a lifelong process that we go through. Some wounds go deeper than even we know. The well of living water instantly springs up in a born-again life, but it takes time and our cooperation to wash us from our own filth completely. It's a conforming, molding process.

I would also like to note that during most of the Jesus People Revival, there seemed to be no real warfare at all. It was there for sure, but God kept us focused on the job at hand, which was "bringing in the sheaves!" Because of his love for us and his desire to spend eternity with each and every one of his children, it was victory after victory during that season of revival!

Kathryn continued to press in, "And the new birth experience is real?"

"Sure is!"

"It's the most real thing in the world?" she asked.

I answered, "He's really, really real!"

As the crowd laughed at my emphasis, Kathryn Kuhlman closed the segment with, "How many of you know what Lonnie is talking about?" People in the studio were affirming the reality of the Son of the living God with joyful laughter and shouts of agreement all over the room.

If anything good comes out of my story, it has to be a revelation that Jesus is real. That is my heart's desire and passion—that you and everyone would discover him. Jesus *is* alive! People who claim there is no evidence of a risen Christ are really the ones looking through blind eyes. They don't even realize that they are blind, but God is reaching out to you with revelation! The Holy Spirit is wooing you to the Savior of your soul. Miracles of life and divine interaction are right in front of your face. Ask, and you shall see.

Open your eyes in the mighty name of Jesus! He is real, and you can personally know him. Touch my testimony and receive him. Jesus says, "Confess me before men, and I will confess you before the angels of heaven and before the very throne of God."[29]

We love you, Daughter of Destiny. **I definitely believe in miracles!**

TEN

Debby

Now I'd like to introduce you to my personal favorite worship leader, Debby Kerner, and have her describe what it was like to travel around with us during this exciting season with Calvary. Debby was raised in a Jewish family, but as a teenager she gave her heart to Jesus, the King of the Jews. The Jesus People movement was in full swing when I first met Debby in 1970, and the Holy Spirit was opening doors that blew all of our minds. We were all just saying *yes* to anything and everything that God was doing, simply going along for the ride—and what a ride it has been!

"*NORMAL CHRISTIAN LIFE*"
by Debby Kerner

Even before I became a Christian, God was preparing me for the worship ministry he was calling me *to* and laying a good foundation *for* me in music. I was a young teenager at the beginning of the folk music revival. I played guitar, wrote music, and was in musicals. In January 1969, I accepted Christ in Palm Springs, California, where I was in high school. I had long straight hair and loved long dresses, but I was not a real hippy. I never lived in the hills or did drugs. Still, I was a part of the Jesus movement. At the beginning, we had Christian houses such as Shiloh, which moved up to Oregon. I was in college in Riverside, where we had the House of Miracles. I used to go over there and play music at their Bible studies. At the beginning of my ministry, I sang in different churches and led worship in several groups, including our local Campus Crusade for Christ. I wrote songs like "Behold I Stand at the Door and Knock" during that time.

In the fall of 1970, Lonnie Frisbee started coming to All Saints Episcopal Church in Riverside on Sunday nights. I came the second Sunday to hear Lonnie and see what was going on. When Lonnie asked, "Do we have any music tonight?" a guy named Fred Waugh stood up and said, "Debby Kerner's here, and she'll play." Fred had helped to get the outreach at All Saints going, but I didn't know Fred then from Adam and Eve. I just looked at him and said, "Well, I will if somebody brought a guitar." Somebody jumped up and exclaimed, "I have one in my car!" and ran out to get it. I sat next to Lonnie on the stage and started singing either "Amen, Praise the Lord" or "Come Walk with Me in the Spirit." When I finished the song, Lonnie fell sideways off his chair. He was such a clown. It was his way of saying, "Wow."

I went to the Waughs' house after the service, and Lonnie came up to me and told me, "You **have** to come to Calvary Chapel."

I answered, "I keep trying to find it, but I get lost in the bean fields." At the time, I was driving an old car with no windshield wipers, a hole in the floorboard, and tires that were coming apart. That's all I had to drive, and I was grateful for it. Gas was somewhere between twenty-five to fifty cents a gallon, and I didn't have any money, so even that amount was expensive. I would pack my car full of people, and sometimes we'd split gas money to go down there. We tried to find Calvary Chapel twice with no success.

Lonnie said, "I'll give you directions and you'll find it, because I want you to come on Wednesday night and lead worship."

So I did. I'd go down and sing, and Lonnie'd usually sing with me. The recordings of us together are hysterical because his voice is so squeaky compared to mine. It wasn't *that* bad, but he just was not a real singer. I didn't know much about performing in a Christian crowd. I thought that the big thing was not to call attention to myself. I didn't even adjust the mic! Nobody applauded; everybody made the "One Way!" sign, pointing one finger toward heaven to give God all the glory.

When I first led worship, there were a couple hundred kids filling the pews and sitting in front. The attendance exploded to several thousand over the next few weeks. I never even thought about it being unusual. To me, that was expected. God had opened a door, and I walked through it, so of course God was going to do amazing stuff. We would start with singing, mostly choruses, sometimes with solos, and often we got to hear from one of the many Christian musical groups that sprung up along with the Jesus People movement. Lonnie would preach, then we prayed for people. Lives were changed. That was our normal. When I finally found my way through the bean fields to Calvary Chapel that first Wednesday night, I had no idea that I would be a part of the unique outpouring of the Holy Spirit there for the next twenty years.

Often Lonnie and I would go to different places together in addition to the Wednesday night service, doing essentially the same format. Lonnie would speak, and I would sing. Calvary Chapel was very active.

Debby Kerner and Lonnie

Pastor Chuck Smith also took me under his wing, and I often sang for Chuck the way I would for Lonnie. I'd lead worship on Monday nights if Chuck asked me. I was continually writing new songs with lots of Scripture or ideas from Scripture in them as they were needed, and the music was always fresh.

With Lonnie, there was a very light spirit about things. He came across as completely genuine. We enjoyed ministering together and being with people. We had a very easy and comfortable relationship. I didn't look at him and see this great, holy, righteous guy. I saw a guy who was fun to be around, but that was because we were likeminded. We wanted to do what God wanted us to do. I knew God had called me to worship and had definitely put a call on my life to follow him. Lonnie had the same call. We were just two Christians coming alongside each other at the right time. It was a God thing that we were working or ministering together. We laughed about as much as we spent time in worship. The laughter was part of the worship experience. It was fellowship. Whether we were enjoying the fellowship we had with others in ministry, sharing Christ, or simply relaxing, the thrust of our direction was that we were to be ministers wherever we were.

We'd pray for people, and I know miracles happened. Reports came back from several people who would tell us they were healed or set free from prisons like drug addiction and destroyed families. I even prayed for a girl with brain cancer, and she was healed. Her doctors were amazed. I was amazed because I don't have the gift of healing. The attitude was just: "We're called, and we're *doing* what we're called to do," and with that came a lot of joy.

It also came with a lot of opportunities to grow in faith. None of us had any money, but God always provided. There was an atmosphere of expectancy toward God's provision for us. Lonnie was a great artist and sold some of his oil paintings. People often gave some kind of a love gift to us, but the provision that covered our daily needs usually came when we did not know it was coming. I loved living in the expectancy that God was going to provide for all our needs and that he was going to show up. I thought miracles were normal and learned to expect to see miracles every day. I'd wake up each morning with the expectancy that God would be guiding me, providing for my needs, and doing something actively in my life. That was normal. It still is.

Some people think miracles are only huge demonstrations of God's intervention, such as the parting of the Red Sea in Exodus. I think we can shift our perspectives a bit to see what God is doing in us and around us each day. The transforming power of the Holy Spirit, who is active every day in our lives, opens the eyes of our hearts to see miracles happening all around us.

I really think what I can say more than anything else about that time with Lonnie is that there was also a spirit of obedience. Our lives were offered to God. When God opened doors for us, we simply walked through them. We weren't afraid. And those doors sometimes opened when we were not expecting anything at all.

Lonnie and Debby on stage

One evening when I was spending the weekend with Lonnie and his wife, Connie, Lonnie really wanted to go to an art fair in Laguna. Connie had some place else to be, so I went with Lonnie. Well, it was the Festival of the Arts, so obviously we couldn't find a place to park. We were like, "What's going on? This town is packed." We spent over half an hour looking for parking and couldn't find a spot anywhere. Lonnie finally turned up a street, winding into the hills. We turned the corner, and there was Oden Fong from the band Mustard Seed Faith in the street, saving a space. He looked really upset.

We asked Oden, "What's going on?"

Oden said, "Come on. You're late. The service has already started."

We were just out looking for parking to go to the art fair! We didn't know there was a service in the hills of Laguna. But again, a door opened, and we walked through. The stage was already set up, and lots of people were sitting around—it was *full*. I don't even remember where I got the guitar from, but somebody handed me a guitar. I went up and sang, Lonnie preached, prayed for people, and

97

then we walked out and went to see some art before going home! We never thought about it. Neither one of us went, "That was weird," or "Didn't expect that." It was normal.

When we got home, Connie was sitting at the kitchen table and asked, "Did Oden find you?"

Lonnie and I looked at each other and went, "What?" Remember, this was before cell phones.

Connie said, "Oden called and called. He was so persistent and said that he was doing a service and that you had to be there tonight. I told him, 'They'll be there if the Lord wants them there.'"

Lonnie and I looked at each other and were both just blown away. It was definitely a hair-raising, "goose bumps" moment—we knew only God could arrange that! Things like that happened a lot as we ministered together.

Lonnie was serious about taking the gospel *everywhere*, so he was excited about receiving a letter from Pastor Stanley Sjoberg in Stockholm, Sweden, inviting Lonnie to come minister at the City Church. Lonnie put a team of six people from Calvary together, including me, to go on the mission to Sweden.

When I told my dad about it, he thought that if his nineteen-year-old daughter was planning to go off to the other side of the world, he was at least going to make sure that she got there in one piece. He wanted to meet Lonnie. It was hysterical. Lonnie drove up in his old used Lincoln Continental with me and Connie in the car. We walked into the house, and my dad looked at the sign on the car that read, "Maranatha." My dad thought it read, "Marijuana." He asked Lonnie, "Why are you driving a car that says *marijuana?*" So there was Lonnie with his long hair and hippy clothing, and I'm sure he looked like Charles Manson to my dad. My father was probably thinking, "What kind of people is my daughter getting involved with?" Then the *Time* magazine with Lonnie on the cover came out. My dad was like, "That's the guy I just had dinner with! What's going on?"

I said, "Dad, it's okay. He's not running a cult or anything like that. We're just going on a mission trip to Sweden."

He looked at me like, "Are you crazy?" But he couldn't stop me, since I wasn't asking him for money but raising money on my own.

One of the exciting things that happened while we were still raising support for our trip was that I got to arrange the music for and sing on the Kathryn Kuhlman show at a large meeting she held at the Hollywood Palladium. Kathryn was really "on fire" and was thoroughly enjoying a meeting with so many young people. I don't remember everything she had Lonnie do, but I do remember that at one point a man from the audience came up for prayer and started falling over when Kathryn laid hands on him. Chuck Smith saw that no one was there to help break his fall, so he jumped up to catch him. More people who came up for prayer started falling over around him, so Chuck kept catching people, which was funny because he felt *really* uncomfortable with people being "slain in the Spirit." In fact, I remember some time earlier Lonnie told me that he'd lose his job at Calvary if people kept falling over, so we'd pray for people and grab them, saying, "Don't fall!" But Chuck was like a father to me—and to Lonnie—and I knew that being a "catcher" was definitely not the job Chuck asked for. I wanted to find a graceful way out for him, so at one of the breaks I decided to stop playing and sat down. Chuck was able to ease out of the action.

Kathryn and I related well with each other. Prior to the Palladium event, she had asked me to travel around the country with her and to be in charge of the music for the youth. I had told her I would pray about it. I was in college, and it would have meant dropping out of school. After taking several weeks to ponder that amazing offer, I decided God had opened the door for me to go to college and that I should finish the course set before me. After the program that evening, Kathryn was elated with how well the Palladium event had gone. She took me backstage with her and spoke with excitement about all the things we would do together around the States. I had to say, "Kathryn, I'm sorry, but I really don't think that's what God wants me to do right now."

My statement caught her by surprise, but she just said, "Oh, okay." I could see what disappointment and obedience looked like in this woman of God. I could also see the wheels in her mind turning.

Finally, she said, "Well, how are you doing on raising money for Sweden?"

I told her, "I'm almost there. Just about four hundred dollars short."

Then she reached into her purse and took out four hundred dollars and gave it to me on the spot. It was a huge lesson for me in humility and generosity. Thanks to her gift, I was able to help other people finish raising their support money.

It was such a beautiful evening. Along with her donation, Kathryn also gave me her corsage, the same one she'd worn that night, which was sweet. I got a professional tip from her as well. I noticed she had a white dress hanging backstage that was identical to the one she was wearing. When I asked her about it, she said, "Think about it. It's white. What if I spill something on it? I have to have something to change into." I thought that was brilliant, and I actually started paying attention to what I wore and how I came across to people at that point, even carrying an extra outfit with me from that time on. I consider Kathryn one of my mentors.

When our team finally raised enough money for the trip, we flew to England, our first stop on the way to Sweden. We all had these heavy backpacks, and it was pretty funny because none of us practiced walking around with them beforehand. We got off the plane, and a friend of mine named Dale met us at the airport. We had no place to stay, so Dale called a friend of his who had an apartment, and we crashed there. We all slept on the floor, which was very common throughout the trip. I remember plenty of times when we'd just roll out our sleeping bags. We took it as it came, and we had fun being together even if we were a bit sore in the morning. The next day we crossed the Channel and took a very *long* train ride with our first-class Eurail passes. That was pretty amusing to the other passengers. Here we were, these scruffy-looking young people on no sleep, with no shower, wearing huge backpacks, all headed to Stockholm, writing songs on the train with no idea what was ahead for us.

When we got to Stockholm, Sweden, the station was filled with people who came to meet us. One of our main Swedish contacts,

Stanley Sjoberg, was there with a lot of people from his church. Stanley said, "Let's pray for Lonnie Frisbee and his group," and he started praying in Swedish and in English for the Holy Spirit to come upon us and bless us, the kind of prayer you would expect from a Pentecostal preacher. It was very powerful. We hadn't known if anybody would show up to meet us, and here were these amazingly fervent and kind people so excited for us to be there. They had a tent meeting going on and said, "We're going to take you to a hotel right near a park where we have a tent set up, and you're going to speak tonight." When we saw the hotel, we were blown away. It was a very upscale place with nice furniture and duvets on *actual* beds. We were like, "This is wonderful! How did we rate this kind of treatment?" We certainly weren't used to living like that and were all definitely grateful for their hospitality.

The first meeting went well, and the people gave us a really good reception. We sang; Lonnie preached. It was simple. The leaders said, "We want you to come back for a second night." So we came back the second night, and it was jammed. The whole park filled up with people, so much so that they had to lift up the sides of the tent. Then the third night we went, and the same thing happened— only bigger, and the press was there.

Lonnie said to us after the third meeting, "They want us to go to churches all over Sweden so that we can preach everywhere."

I said, "Well, we've got Eurail passes, why not?"

So we went up north, down south, everywhere. We went to Gothenburg, Linköping, and many other

From left to right: Lonnie, Connie, Jim Golden, and Debby Kerner in Sweden

cities. Reporters started traveling on the train with us. Huge churches and sports stadiums were arranged for us to be able to continue sharing the gospel. Sometimes the team would split up to be able to cover both a stadium and a church at the same time. Swedish brothers and sisters would shuttle us back and forth between venues. Thousands of people accepted Christ as their Savior at these meetings. Sometimes the Christians would sing to us after we had sung to them. The beauty of that is etched in my memory. This went on for about two weeks to a month.

One particular famous Swedish singer was a Christian, and she began to travel with us. Swedish television stations got involved, and

Jesusfolket är här

lots of publicity surrounded us. It was a phenomenal time. Years later a Swedish friend of mine showed me a high school textbook from her Swedish school. In it was a picture of me wearing this granny dress, with Lonnie and other team members making the "One Way!" sign. The caption said, "A finger to the sky is the new sign." It was an article about how our time in Sweden was the biggest revival in Swedish history. It was *amazing*. Literally, places were so full that people would try to climb through or sit in open windows in these big churches just to hear us.

One night our team was ministering in a huge Cathedral and in a giant outdoor sports arena at the same time, and *both* venues were full. Again, our hosts shuttled us between the two locations so that we could be at both places live. Lonnie would give an altar call, and people would just bolt out of their seats. I gave it on some occasions because the team would be split in different spots. We would pray with people for a long time after our services. We even learned a few Swedish phrases so we could reach out to the Swedes in their own language.

We rode first class around the country, singing on the trains, meeting people from all over the world, finding out about their lives, and of course, sharing the Good News. It was normal stuff for us, and yet it was so supernaturally huge. I look back wondering, "How did that happen?" Simple answer: The Holy Spirit made it happen. Not one of us in our own strength had the know-how or the capability to do that. There was a sovereign work of God going on at that time, and all we had to do was say, "Yes, we'll be there." I've been back to Sweden many times since then, and it is so interesting to see the impact of that first trip we went on over there.

After our mission to Sweden, we returned to London. We were invited to a meeting in a large hall near Westminster Abbey and Parliament. There were several bishops and priests on the stage, all wearing their long cassocks that looked like dresses to people unfamiliar with clerical robes. Lonnie sat on the stage with them. At first it was like, "Well, who's this long-haired hippy walking into this situation with these theological experts," but they were all pretty nice. The religious leaders did not put Lonnie down. They were quite kind and polite. Our team sat in the audience, surrounded by a bunch of people who were throwing tomatoes at these guys. I had never seen anything like that. It was pretty entertaining.

Later I was asked to sing at the first ever Festival of Light in Hyde Park. There were approximately eighty thousand people in the crowd. When it was my turn to go on the stage, just as I started singing, it started to rain. I thought, "Oh well. That's it. They're going to go home." But the people didn't react that way. They knelt down—eighty thousand people knelt in the rain—and I looked around from the stage, going, "Wow, Lord!" It was a powerful example of the Holy Spirit falling upon God's people. My nineteen-year-old brain was in awe. I had no idea what a huge movement the Festival of Light would become.

It was my privilege to minister with Lonnie for about a year. When I recall that time, I've said that being with Lonnie was like living in the Book of Acts. That is not an exaggeration. It really was. But I thought that was normal Christian life. We were doing things like Christians had done in the Bible, so why shouldn't it be normal?

It didn't even strike me as being all that extraordinary. The extraordinary was ordinary, and it was very, very cool. We loved the surprises that came, and we saw God be faithful over and over again. It was very spontaneous and born out of hearts that just wanted to please God, hearts that said *yes*. And that really was what Lonnie was all about, who he was at his core.

ELEVEN

Deliverance

IN THE BEGINNING of the revival, not only did we see a flood of salvations, but we also discovered a huge need for people to be delivered from all kinds of bondages. Some of them were as small as being addicted to cigarettes or pot and some as severe as full-on demonic possession. Drugs and the occult had a huge impact on the flower-power generation.

Deliverance ministry is a very messy business and extremely controversial. Many Christians, not to mention most of secular society, don't really believe demonic entities are at work in people's lives. People don't believe the Bible either, which clearly declares that we have authority in the name of Christ over these forces of darkness. However, I have experienced countless encounters where people have been delivered, healed, and totally restored by a powerful touch of the Holy Spirit when we actually spoke and commanded those dark entities to leave and stop their destruction in the name of Jesus. There is still a lot of work needed after a person is set free, but it is a beautiful thing to see a brother or sister come alive with a fresh sparkle, a new light in their eyes.

In Newport Beach we had the halfway house called the Bluetop Motel. It had been a house of prostitution during World War II, or a "house of ill repute," as some would call it. It is probably the oldest structure in Newport and became one of our Calvary Chapel communities. It had nine units. City and county hotlines would work with us because we accepted people off the street, provided them food and lodging, and of course, we did the good old General Booth thing: soup, soap, and the gospel. It was definitely a 24/7 labor of love and hard work. It was non-stop, believe me.

So one day a phone call came in from a young man named Gary. Gary talked to me on the phone and said that he was in terrible desperation and needed help. He was friendly enough and

105

seemed to be sincerely seeking help. I tested him with questions. We didn't just take in anybody, because we wanted to keep a family atmosphere. We had mostly young singles in our community along with a married couple or two. We also had small children in the mix. There was a ton of interaction. It was a compact Christian commune. In other words, we tried not to do things that would upset family peace.

So anyway, Gary had been referred to us by an outside organization, a telephone hotline. He came, and we fed him dinner. He was nice in conversation. He covered his teeth with his upper lip by bringing it down over his teeth. You could see that he was embarrassed about having bad teeth and was trying to cover them up.

As we were sitting there having a conversation, suddenly something very evil manifested itself upon him. It seemed to grip him right at the kitchen table, and he slowly said in a deep, guttural voice, "This is really me talking." The devil was in his eyes. I'll never forget the shock that hit me as he said, "This is really me talking."

Then he totally blew our minds. Gary went backwards out of the kitchen chair, where he had been sitting to eat with us, and rolled in an arch onto the floor. I lie not. A spirit definitely manifested. Before he hit the kitchen floor, he rolled into another somersault. He did two flips out of the chair, one flip right after another. Then he started bouncing around like a fish in the bottom of a boat. White foam came out of his entire mouth like a mad dog, and his lips went back like a chimpanzee's. He folded back his mouth to expose totally rotten teeth, teeth that were rotten up to the gums and hadn't been brushed for a long period of time. An odor began to come from him that was pungent and overpowering. The only other time I ever smelled anything similar was a few years later in Africa when a hundred-pound male baboon sat on our air-conditioning unit. It was the smell of an animal. When total possession comes on people, their bodies deteriorate because their demons are there to kill them. They hate the people they are possessing. There are usually foul odors, bad hygiene, bad language. It was intense as we watched him flopping on the floor.

So then this demon got up like a wild tiger and came charging at me. Out of his mouth came threats of murder. It was as if a wild animal was pouncing on me. He ran across the room with a full fist raised up. All I could see was this fist coming. In one long motion, he swung back his arm, as I instinctively prepared to fend off a blow. He fired his fist toward my face, but it stopped two inches before he made contact. Praise God for the Holy Ghost. Praise God for the angels of heaven, because not only did he immediately stop like his fist hit a brick wall, but he became paralyzed, stiff like a board, and fell like a tree being cut down: stiff, straight, back on the ground.

I said, "I am the servant of the Most High God, and you *must* obey me. Identify who you are!"

The spirit identified itself. I forget which ancient name he had, but I got the identification of the spirit. I used the authority that the Lord gave me in his name, as well as the thousands of people in the ministry behind me in agreement, you know, saints in our ministry who were secretly backing my authority with their prayers of agreement during the revival. The Bible says, "One can fight a thousand, but two can fight ten thousand."[30] In addition to the earthly battle, we have a great cloud of witnesses in heaven. With that authority, I spoke to that spirit, commanding, "It's time for you to go out of him in the mighty name of Jesus Christ of Nazareth!" I cast the spirit out with a word, and that man was completely and totally set free!

Let me give a word of caution here to Christians. You do not lay hands in prayer on demonized people like some suggest. It is not even biblical. You speak and command the spirits to come out with the authority God gives us in the name of Jesus. The Bible goes on to say, "Rejoice not, that the spirits are subject unto you; but rather rejoice, because your names are written in heaven."[31]

Gary was set free and immediately became part of our community. He got born from above. We scrubbed him down, got him a haircut, and loved on him with the unconditional love of Christ. However, we did more than that, more than just a haircut. We did more than he could ever have expected. We took him to a clinic and had all of his teeth fixed. We got him a job, and we brought him to Bible studies. He turned out to be one of the most precious brothers in our community of believers.

Gary later told us his story. When he was a little boy, he was lying on his bed one night when suddenly a dark cloud came over him. An audible voice spoke out of the cloud and asked permission to enter into him. As a child, he gave permission for that spirit to enter. From that time on, from the age of about twelve years old, the spirit possessed him. It came, spoke, and he gave it permission to enter.

People need to wake up to the reality of a demonic realm. It is more than Linda Blair in a Hollywood thriller. But more importantly, people need to *experience* the reality of a Savior who conquered all of the works of darkness, including death. That is the bottom line.

Gary became a very beautiful believer after we got him cleaned up and into a routine—along with some good homemade cooking in his belly—and, most importantly, after he got himself all straightened out with God! What a wonderful testimony!

LACY

Here's one of my very favorite true stories. Serving God has so many interesting twists and turns. Some can be exhilarating, some can come in the form of trials and tribulations, and others can be absolutely mind-blowing. My encounter with a young woman named Lacy falls into the mind-boggling category. This story might even sound like fiction because the demonic realm has been so cleverly masked or hidden with other explanations. However, multiple eyewitnesses were present for everything that I'm reporting. In fact, there were over a hundred eyewitnesses present in this one dramatic episode alone.

At Calvary Chapel we would take turns manning the phones because we were ministering to thousands of people and there was always so much to do. Most people don't realize how challenging it can be to truly meet the needs of a church or a community. As a leader in even a small church, it can consume your life, so you better be sure of your calling to lead and be sure that your motives are right with God or else you will be very frustrated. You will actually become more of a hindrance than a blessing.

Anyway, I was working as a phone counselor one day, and the phone rang. I answered with, "God bless you, Calvary Chapel."

There was a silent pause as I waited for a response, and then— *click*. Someone hung up the phone.

The phone rang again.

"God bless you, Calvary Chapel."

Click.

Then it rang again.

"God bless you, Calvary Chapel."

Click.

I can't remember how many times the phone rang, but it was multiple times—*click, click, click*. Later we found out it was a lady named Lacy who was heavily involved in witchcraft in Southern California. To Lacy, her involvement in witchcraft was an innocent thing in the beginning, starting with horoscopes or asking a Ouija board questions about her unhappy marriage, things like that. Slowly she was drawn into the occult and into deep spiritual bondage. Lacy eventually became a practicing witch and even belonged to a witch's coven in Orange County, California. By the way, Southern California has a lot of witches.

Lacy was going to receive her robe and ring and drink blood in a ceremony to gain even more power in witchcraft. In preparation for this upcoming high-level event, she had a vision. In the vision she saw a number: 5402941.

She had no idea what that number represented, so she went to her Ouija board and began to work her magic. Her Ouija board spelled out: "I T M E A N S Y O U R D E A T H," which would prove to be pretty prophetic.

Lacy freaked out and decided to try dialing that number on the phone since there were seven digits in the number like a normal phone line. How totally shocked she was to hear me say, "God bless you, Calvary Chapel." She was speechless and just hung up. She called again several times, trying to get some information, but each time, she couldn't talk and just hung up. Finally, she got through to one of the other extensions and found out what we were and where we were. How amazing that she had a radiant vision of my telephone number, which was actually the church's phone number.

There is a clear example in the Bible of the satanic prophesying truth. A slave girl "possessed with a spirit of divination" followed Paul and his company around. She kept crying out, "These men are the servants of the Most High God, who proclaim to us the way of salvation." She kept it up for several days, until Paul got "greatly annoyed," turned to the spirit, and said, "I command you in the name of Jesus Christ to come out of her!"[32] It says the demon came out of her immediately. Read the story. It is very interesting.

Lacy was supernaturally given my phone number, and then she drove to Costa Mesa to our address. When she arrived, she could not turn the steering wheel of her car into the parking lot of the church. Instead, she drove around the block and came back around at least five times, unsuccessfully trying to enter the parking lot. She was absolutely hysterical and totally believed that her life was in the balance. Finally, with all of her might, she was able to enter the lot and park. However, she quickly discovered that she couldn't get out of her car. The powers of darkness that had slowly captured her over a period of years were desperately and powerfully trying to take over and keep her away.

Somebody in the office noticed a woman absolutely freaking out in a car. An assistant pastor and I looked out the window and saw a woman trying to get out of her car. She was crying and making all sorts of wild motions inside her vehicle. It looked like she was definitely in desperate trouble. The pastor and I went out, and I opened the car door. The woman looked up at me, and I was shocked. She had shaved her eyebrows off and painted on these real wicked looking witch eyebrows. Most shocking of all were her eyeballs themselves. They were dancing like the flames of a candle, only each eye was dancing to a different rhythm. I have never seen anybody's eyeballs do what her eyes were doing. They were flickering like candles, but they weren't doing it together. It was a mesmerized look, like one a moth must have as it flies toward a flame. When I saw her eyes dancing around, I knew that she was definitely possessed by a powerful spirit. I had not seen evidence of such an overwhelming demonic presence since working in the Haight-Ashbury with some of Anton LaVey's cohorts. In the Living Room we saw people totally set free from the grip of "His Satanic Majesty."

And so I reached down to take hold of this woman, and she started to scream. Every time I touched her, she screamed. It caused her pain, as if she were being burned. At least I discovered that I could torment the spirit inside of her. The touch of a saint can cause extreme pain to a demonized person because of the presence of the Holy Spirit operating in the child of God. If the Holy Spirit is active anywhere around a demon, it will manifest. If you are walking down the street under the anointing of God, demons often manifest. That happened several times to me later in Africa.

Again I took hold of her arm. She was screaming bloody murder as we led her into the prayer room inside the church. She immediately grabbed a Bible on the table and shredded it like the popular Power Team would rip apart phone books. With a loud cackling noise like a witch would sound on Halloween, she threw the Bible into the air and tore it into shreds. As one of the pastors and I were watching the Bible float down like snowflakes in the sky, I loudly said to her, "The Scriptures say that heaven and earth will pass away, but his words will never pass away. Now get the hell out of her in the name of Jesus!"

That spirit came tearing out of her like a wounded dog, but not before she manifested almost total possession, falling to the ground, foaming at the mouth, and distorting her face and features. But at our command, she was set free. She really got gloriously delivered, but she was not *totally* free yet. There were more spirits involved, more bondage, more work to be done.

I was only allowed to give each person forty-five minutes in my counseling sessions. It was one of my disappointments as the church grew, multiplied, and became more sophisticated, organized, and sanitized. Deliverance ministry was definitely not encouraged. So I discreetly had Lacy book for the upcoming week for further

111

deliverance. What God allowed in this situation with Lacy was that he put her deliverance on hold until the next time she could have an appointment with me.

At our next appointment, Lacy came in and immediately manifested again. Lacy tore another Bible up just like that. It was shocking and got the adrenaline pumping real quick. For me, it was "been there, done that!" I guess the spirits were just trying to make a demonstration as if they were destroying the Word of God.

I want you to know that I, Lonnie Frisbee, am not a demon chaser. I have met people who are enthralled with deliverance. I believe that if a spirit is challenging you right before your eyes, then it's best to hit the enemy straight on and take that battle. And yet there was a period of time in my ministry when I dealt with one demon-possessed person after another, after another, after another. We were dealing with demon-possessed people sometimes hourly.

People eventually heard that we moved in deliverance, and they came from far away to be set free. If God gives you a deliverance ministry, pray he will deliver you from deliverance. There is so much more to the Christian experience than spiritual warfare. Deliverance can get very messy, as you might be detecting. Nevertheless, these precious people like Lacy desperately need help, and God has given us the tools and the authority. You can believe it or not.

Let me pause from Lacy's story and give you a previous example of why Calvary Chapel frowned on deliverance at the church. I got a call to come over to the office one day and was told that there was a demon-possessed person, a member of the church, who needed help. A man's wife had apparently become totally possessed. It was as if she had a nervous breakdown and a spirit had taken her over. She and her husband were waiting for me in the office.

When I arrived, it looked to me like the devil was actually controlling the bodily functions of this person. I never saw any woman move like she did. She was in her mid-fifties and was dancing around like little Sheba, like a belly dancer. She was twirling and twisting with sensuality and seduction. She fell onto the ground and started moving like a very large serpent across the floor. We watched the muscles of her stomach go in and out like how a real snake would crawl along. It was shocking. I saw hell in her eyes.

One of the residing elders of the church was standing there praying against the spirit, and before we realized what was happening, she slithered over to him like a giant python and quickly reached up to his crotch. He tried to stop her, but she managed to fight and grab hold of him in one motion, prophesying that he was committing adultery. It happened very quickly. To the elder's shame, he was taken in adultery a short time later.

Now, when you have a deliverance ministry and the demons won't obey your voice, you call 911. That's what happened. Before we could do anything else to deal with this person, one of the pastors called 911. The lady got up off the floor and tried to jump through the pastor's window in his office. She thrust herself across the room and went flying into a huge plate-glass window. She literally jumped up in the air as if she were superman trying to fly away. However, the thick glass bounced her back off the window, and the paramedics came shortly thereafter. They put her in a straitjacket and took her to a mental institution for evaluation.

The church issued a new rule: no more deliverance ministry. Like I mentioned already, deliverance can be messy. I understand that, but the new rule was very unfortunate. I did not want to be rebellious, but I would sometimes do deliverance in the janitor's closet after that rule was announced. I don't know if it is still a rule in the hundreds of Calvary Chapels around the world today. I pray not. Jesus cast out demons all the time in his earthly ministry. One of the gifts of the Spirit of God in the Bible is the discernment of spirits. So granted, not every case is demonic, but there would be no reason to deal with demons at all if God didn't call us to have authority over the satanic realm or if it weren't real. Scripture clearly says that Jesus has given us authority over all the works of the devil and that he'll make our enemies our footstool.[33]

However, new believers should not immediately jump into deliverance ministry, not until they are knowledgeable in the Word of God and have their feet firmly planted in a solid walk in the kingdom of God with Jesus Christ as Lord and head. *Then* "these signs shall follow them that believe. In my name shall they cast out devils...."[34] That is a promise, a fact.

Now back to Lacy's story, which was an unauthorized deliverance session a year or so after this other dramatic incident in the pastor's office. Lacy was delivered from three major spirits at the command of the Lord. They identified themselves, sometimes speaking in ancient names. If you traced what these spirits were saying, they would use names that stemmed out of Greek mythology and things like that, names like Apollyon and Odysseus. You see, these lying spirits have been around for thousands of years, and they like to prey on weak souls. We saw Lacy set free in our second meeting, but once again, we did not have enough time to deal with all the captivity in her life.

The battle can be very intense and time-consuming. Often it can take hours. Many ministers who know about and have even successfully experienced deliverance encounters are too lazy or selfish to change their schedule to deal with a situation. There is also another factor in some battles. Jesus explained, some particular demons "only come out by prayer and fasting." Each case can be radically different.

Lacy's final deliverance happened like this. It was our third session. I decided to bring her into my Afterglow service that I conducted after the main meeting on Wednesday nights. I would always conduct Afterglows for people to go deeper and to receive the baptism of the Holy Spirit. The importance of knowing and receiving all that the Spirit has to offer is one of the absolute top priorities of my life and ministry. The empowering of the Holy Spirit had such an impact on me that I want everyone to experience that blessing and power.

We had close to a hundred spiritually hungry people, out of the thousands who attended the main service, who would come into the Afterglow meetings each week. I figured, "Why not let the saints pray for Lacy and see her really set free!" Remember, the Bible says, "One can fight a thousand, two can fight ten thousand."[35] How about a hundred? How about a whole church or a whole nation of believers? After all, we are theoretically a Christian nation here in

America. Right? We could set entire nations free, including our own, if we would just come together in unity and exercise our authority in Christ's name!

It made sense to me, so I set a chair in the front. We arranged for Lacy to be there. She wanted to be totally set free from the devil, but she wasn't yet. So there she was, sitting in the chair in front of the crowd. She was motionless, and a voice was speaking through her mouth even though she was not moving her lips. Her mouth was open, but the voice came from the throat without her moving her mouth at all. She looked like a wax figure. Very frightening. But you're not supposed to be afraid when you're casting out devils. Only the Lord can provide the boldness and confidence at times like this.

I had everybody agree with me for Lacy's deliverance, and then I prayed. We all agreed in Jesus' name and commanded all demonic spirits to leave. The final spirit thrust Lacy's head forward and snapped her long hair like a horse's tail. She went limp…and then she was free, gloriously set free!

The next morning she came to Calvary Chapel's office at about 9:30 a.m. and waited for me to get out of a long staff prayer meeting. Finally, we met. She was radiant, really, but it was the radiance of being swept clean. Don't mistake a clean vessel as a born-again person. You know, Jesus warned, "When an unclean spirit goes out of a man, he goes through dry places, seeking rest, and finds none. Then he says, 'I will return to my house from which I came.' And when he comes, he finds *it* empty, swept, and put in order. Then he goes and takes with him seven other spirits more wicked than himself, and they enter and dwell there; and the last *state* of that man is worse than the first."[36]

Lacy was radiant because she was no longer oppressed by the devil. But like it says, after the house has been swept clean, if you don't accept the Lord, then the enemy will come again with even more demons, and the final state of a person will be worse than it was before. Can you imagine?

Lacy beamed as she told me, "I feel free from the evil, Lonnie."

Right away I saw an opportunity to move in and land Lacy, get another notch on my gospel gun, and brand an "L.F." next to her name. We can unfortunately get overly excited about a victory, when it's really all about Jesus declaring, "Follow me, and I will make you fishers of men."[37] I saw her spirit free and open and ready, and like a used car salesman with an ambition to make a lot of money that week, I almost moved in for the signing of the contract, as it were.

Then the Holy Spirit said, "No! No! Tell Lacy to go and sit on the grass mound out in the front lawn. Have her read the Gospel of John, and *then* tell her how to accept me."

So I said, "Lacy, you go read the Gospel of John and then pray in your own way and ask the Lord to take over your life."

She did it! Lacy got born again. She became a totally new creation in Christ Jesus. "Lacy the witch" was dead, just like her magic board predicted. No more shredding Bibles, screeching like a cat, or manifesting rude, obnoxious behavior. Lacy became my personal secretary for eleven years. She was set free—"Not by might, nor by power, but by my Spirit, saith the Lord!"

TWELVE

Lasting Fruit

I'M PRETTY SURE that each and every person on earth would like their life to count for something. For me, I'll say it again: I am dedicated to Romans 8:14, "As many as are led by the Spirit of God, they are the sons of God."[38] It says we are created for *his* pleasure. I want to please God, don't you? I have discovered that "divine guidance," being led by the Spirit of God, is the number one key. The Holy Spirit within us (*if* you are born again) is the "master key" that opens or closes all doors. He is our guide, teacher, and comforter. He teaches us about Jesus the God-man, the redeemer of mankind, who became one of us. He gives us gifts along with wisdom and revelation. He is God the Spirit leading us to God the Son to the glory of God the Father.

To me, it will all come together when I ultimately hear him say, "Well done, thou good and faithful servant."[39] That moment alone will indeed be the fulfillment of a life that counts for something. In the meantime, Jesus clearly lays it all out for us down here:

Remain in me, as I also remain in you. No branch can bear fruit by itself; it must remain in the vine. Neither can you bear fruit unless you remain in me. I am the vine; you are the branches. If you remain in me and I in you, you will bear much fruit; apart from me you can do nothing.[40]

HARBOR HIGH SCHOOL

During the revival in 1971, everything was going well for the ministry. Every day there were miracles. We were running our homes and halfway houses and doing all kinds of evangelistic outreaches. In addition, we had Bible studies going in four major high schools *on campus*, which is now unheard of in "liberated" America. Our Bible study at Harbor High School (where my aunt had written the alma mater) had up to 150 kids who I, along with Ray Rent of Bethesda Fellowship, had led to Christ in Costa Mesa.

It was near the end of the school year, and God had been visiting us in the science room. I will never forget the anointing that was on those meetings. People will absolutely not believe what was happening in that public school. It was off the scale. The science room was quite large, and the kids would pack in, as word had spread around the campus about the meetings. Sometimes the power of God would descend on everyone, and all of the kids would fall on the ground under the power of the Holy Spirit.

How can anyone orchestrate something like that? It was incredible and very supernatural. They would be speaking in tongues—until the bell would ring for the next class to come in. This did not just happen once. There were many days at Harbor High School when the power of God struck everyone in the room, and we were *all* caught up in the Spirit, praying, seeing visions, and interceding for people to be saved!

I took the Bible study in that direction, but it was definitely all about God's presence. It was so precious to hear the genuine, heartfelt prayers that went up to the Lord from those young lives. They were praying for their friends, their boyfriends and girlfriends, and their family members. So many kids gave their hearts to Jesus and were born again during that time. It was wonderful. The bell would ring, and the kids would still be lying under the power of the Holy Spirit all over the floor everywhere! It was mind-blowing to see that kind of raw power fall on the students. No way could I or any other human orchestrate that kind of scenario. Critics have accused me of crowd manipulation and mass hypnosis, but no way. It was the manifest presence of God! Just ask the people what they experienced.

It was a good thing that we had a comrade in the ranks. The science teacher who had the class the next hour after our meeting was a Spirit-filled Lutheran. He covered for me when the power of God hit the kids. He wouldn't tell what we were up to. He was our

Lutheran doorman, and he was such a saint. I just remember that he was always very appreciative of what was going on. He loved God and was as thrilled as I was to see an outpouring of God's presence on the kids.

These meetings in the science room were in preparation for us to do an outside meeting, but I didn't know it. We were just talking about the kingdom and the Spirit and the power. We would always talk about things that Kathryn Kuhlman talked about, because she taught me about the Holy Spirit, which is why this book is dedicated to her. As I mentioned before, Chuck Smith taught me in the Word, and Kathryn Kuhlman taught me in the Holy Spirit.

One particular day at Harbor High School, a very anointed and very fine young man was converted. It was ninety degrees outside, maybe hotter. Nature was cooperating with a plan. God never does anything without a reason. If you want to know about what God is up to, then look into nature. His design is built into everything. It was late May or early June, and the students were getting ready to graduate from high school. We had one of those occasional Southern California heat waves. Everyone decided that the science room was simply way too hot to meet in with way too many people crammed together in the heat. Like I said, there were well over a hundred students.

I heard the Lord say, "Lonnie, today I want you to go outside. I want you to have an open-air meeting on the lawn."

It was against the law to do an open-air meeting at a public school. I knew that. At the same time, it wasn't really enforced as much back then as it is today, with demonically inspired ACLU lawyers and godless judges coming out of the woodwork.

For that matter, as a little side note, it was also against the law to pass out tracts down at the pier with a group of people or to speak anywhere in public without a permit. I found that out a couple of times. Regardless, I would still occasionally take a bunch of spiritual little babes, who were like little ducklings following their mommy single file into the water, to places like the Huntington Beach pier to "fish for men." We would all cleverly stand there like a human net and watch the crowds of people pass by. We were then able to notice people we could witness to. In that way, we were able to pray and lead many souls to Christ.

One evening two police cars and a helicopter came to arrest us. You know, Huntington Beach did not want a bunch of Jesus freaks witnessing on the pier.

I yelled, "Gee, the cops!"

On cue, everybody spun around in opposite directions, something like in the movie *West Side Story*. We all turned into Joe Citizens, and nobody could mark the leader. Each of us just went off whistling to the sky like we were totally innocent.

So back to Harbor High School on that extremely hot afternoon. There was a young student who was working on building a certain reputation at the school. Some said he was a small-time pot dealer, but rumors are rumors. Our group was on the lawn area, and I was preaching the gospel like Peter on the day of Pentecost. Believe me! It was like the day of Pentecost. The believers were standing all around, and I stood in the midst. I began to open my mouth, and the anointing of God was on me—I'm telling you!

In the background I could hear someone saying things like, "So you think you know it all, huh?" Little railing accusations from a brat came flying at me. He said rude things, and then he began to mock openly. It was like when mosquitoes come around your head: Swatting them away is not the same thing as getting them with a bug zapper. I started to lose my train of thought because he was spewing disrespectful, blasphemous things.

Then the Lord said, "Stretch forth thy hand, and with the authority I have placed on your life, bring him down."

So I did exactly what the Lord said. I stretched forth my hand and used the authority that God put in my words, and I turned everything that he was saying around on him in divine judgment. He fell on the ground, powerless. Before everyone, God struck him with his power and presence. The young student, Greg Laurie, was saved that day, and God also baptized him with the Holy Spirit. It was dramatic.

Subsequently, God raised him up to be a pastor at the age of nineteen years old. He was seventeen when he was converted, and two years later, he was raised up to pastor Harvest Christian Fellowship in Riverside, CA, (from a group I started at All Saints Episcopal Church, which is right down the street from the present church location). Harvest has grown tremendously, and Greg Laurie still pastors one of the largest churches in America. Harvest Christian Fellowship, the first Calvary Chapel offspring, is an excellent evangelistic church and Bible-teaching center, which I highly recommend.

But I'm telling you that back on that hot day at Harbor High School, Greg Laurie got converted when he was struck by the power of God. He was struck down a mocker, but raised up a son of God. It was a very powerful Saul of Tarsus type of conversion with an experience literally from the sky. He became my little brother and spiritual son from that day forward. We were together almost every day while God had him in my school. Greg knew my schedule and followed me everywhere. He spent time with my family and came to my meetings.

In the very beginning of his walk, Greg became the famous cartoonist who invented the Living Water tracts. He did cartoon tracts, and that was his introduction to an amazing career of serving God. Chuck and Kay Smith immediately adopted him as a gifted leader and continued to work closely with him ever since.

I'm recognizing Greg Laurie as a spiritual son who went on to have great success independently of my decisions in his life. It's really important that people find their individual priesthoods like Greg did and not be controlled by headquarters. Otherwise, the anointing of God cannot have freedom. Many say that Greg is like a young Billy Graham, with the thousands of people coming to a saving knowledge of our Lord through his ministry. Greg recently packed out Anaheim Stadium with over sixty thousand people in one of his huge Harvest Crusades. Greg Laurie was the son I never had, and it was "not by might, nor by power, **but by my spirit, saith the Lord!**"[41]

This reminds me of a story that I must tell about a prayer partner God gave me in the early days of the Jesus People movement. He was a friend and a good Christian brother named Blair. We met on a bus on the first foreign mission that Kenn Gulliksen and I, along with a team, were taking to Europe. Kenn later became the founder of Vineyard Christian Fellowship. Underline this in red: Kenn Gulliksen is the founder of the Vineyard. I don't want to confuse anybody, but that's the truth.[42]

Anyway, Kenn and I were on a bus in Europe when I met Blair. Blair was a barber and attended Calvary Chapel of Costa Mesa. On that mission trip, he and I went out on the streets together. We were mission partners, witnessing for Christ two by two, just as the Lord sent them out in the Gospels.

We would simply ask others for decisions and—wow! People would just start asking Christ into their hearts. They began coming to the main meetings we were having every night. It was so cool. We worked the streets of Denmark in the daytime, while it was snowing and super cold, and then did the meetings each evening. We were in Europe for the first time, suffering culture shock and jet lag, but praise God, we brought in souls together!

By the time we arrived back from the mission, a special bonding had taken place. It's kind of like when you go on an exciting hunting or fishing trip with someone, except we had been fishing for men. Blair and I decided that we would seek the Lord early in the morning every other day. Now, I normally didn't get up at 5:30 a.m., but I would get up early and drive from Newport Beach, where my wife and I were directors of the Blue Top Motel, all the way to Blair's place in Huntington Beach.

I would arrive, and Blair would have hot herbal tea all prepared. It was the first time I ever drank herbal tea. He would be waiting for me at the door with a hot cup each morning. According to Scripture, "Those that seek me early shall find me."[43] You know, "seek me *early*." God often puts conditions on things to demonstrate truths and principles for our own good.

For example, the condition for the Jews in the wilderness was to collect their fresh blessing from God every day. Let me give a short little teaching on this. God said that they were to collect manna fresh every day. He connected their food source to his fellowship. Let me repeat that: He connected their food source to his fellowship, just like he connected his covenant to the foreskin of the penis and circumcision. He goes right for what counts with his people. Does that make sense?

And so God said, "You shall gather the fresh blessing that I have for you every morning."[44] It was miraculous, fresh provision from heaven. Through Moses, the Israelites were instructed to collect only enough manna for each day and no more. However, on the sixth day they were to collect enough for two days because they were to devote the Sabbath day to resting in his presence.

God put a wonderful flavor into this manna. If the health food industry had the secret recipe for God's manna, they would become incredibly wealthy. They'd be trillionaires! It had all the right nutrition in it, perfectly balanced nutrition. It tasted like honey and wheat. It cooked up into a wonderful little bread representing the Lord and the loving substance of God. It was perfect.

However, some of the Jews developed a scoundrel attitude. They didn't see that the food was connected to the daily freshness of God's fellowship. They were more focused on their own stomachs and their own convenience. They started to have a bad spirit within them and disobeyed God by collecting more manna than for just one day. One neighbor saw the other one doing it, and soon it spread throughout the whole camp, this disobedience of collecting more manna than was directed.

So God caused worms to be brought forth in the extra manna, and the camp stunk to high heaven. But the extra manna collected on the sixth day, on the day that God gave them permission in preparation for the Lord's Sabbath, that extra manna did not decay. It was kept safe and blessed in the boundaries of obedience. So it is in every area of our lives. He blesses us within the boundaries of obedience and love. Thank God for his New Testament grace revealed through his Son!

Anyway, in addition to overseeing the community and doing outreaches and mission trips, I also preached to over a thousand people every Wednesday night. I *definitely* needed prayer and fresh manna, which is why I started to seek God's presence early in the morning with my friend Blair. He loved the Lord so much, and I was absolutely focused on the Lord and what he was doing in my meetings at Calvary Chapel. So when Blair and I began to seek the Lord's face, immediately the power of the Holy Spirit lifted us up into spheres of light. There was no doubt that both of us were experiencing the same thing! I'm so sorry that I forgot the brand of tea that we were drinking, but I don't think that had anything to do with it.

I remember so vividly having this total sensation of being pulled

upward, as if I had another form inside of me pulling me right through the top of my head. It actually felt like I was shooting out of the top of my head and going into spheres of what apparently was battle. It was incredible. The only way I can describe it is that we would **burst** through dimensions and come into the presence of the Lord. Together we experienced coming into the throne room of God in prayer. Ha ha! What a joy! We are priests after the order of Melchizadek!

"SURFS UP"

There was another young man I became close to who came to the Lord through Calvary Chapel's ministry. His name is Danny Lehmann. We went overseas on mission trips with Calvary Chapel teams and did other things like that. He was what they called a "gremmie." Back then, a "gremmie" was a young surfer, the kind who liked Teenage Mutant Ninja Turtles. Danny was a towheaded surfer who had a pet dog with a bandana around his neck. He lived for surfing. But the Lord really got a major hold on Danny the surfer dude.

I remember he made an appointment to meet with me, and I came to his house for dinner. He said, "Well, do you want to eat and then pray and read the Bible, or do you want to pray and read the Bible and then eat?"

I said, "Why don't we pray and read the Bible before we eat, and then we'll pray and read the Bible after we eat too." I knew he was just interested in praying and reading the Bible and fellowshipping. He didn't want to do anything else but that. His whole life was just completely caught up in fellowshipping with people who loved Jesus, in reading the Word, and staying in prayer. He was definitely "hanging ten" with Jesus all the way.

One time Danny and I checked out a large secular outdoor festival. I did my street thing and witnessed for Christ to a growing crowd that gathered around. At a certain point I said, "This is my friend Danny, and he'd like to share a few things with you now." I put him right on the spot. It was his ministry debut and the first time he publicly shared his faith. He did great!

Danny Lehmann later became the director of Youth with a Mission, or YWAM, in Honolulu. We have had a lot of history together over the years. He even married a girl in a church I helped start. We go way back. Out of all of the people I ever had an influence on and got to watch his walk with Jesus, Danny Lehmann has made me the proudest. He trains third-world missionaries and is a dynamo for God! He's the author of several books, travels all around the world, and is absolutely power-packed when he speaks. I am very proud of him, a "gremmie" for Jesus.

Greg Laurie and Danny were similar in their need for a father. Tom Stipe also fits in that category. So this is the gathering-in of the fatherless generation. Greg Laurie and Danny Lehmann are people who have gone on to marry, start families, and lead very large and successful ministries.

"THE SIDE OF MY HEAD IS BLOWN OFF"

On one of the Wednesday night meetings at Calvary Chapel, the place was again completely packed out. Chuck Girard and Love Song had just blessed our socks off with their talent and totally original music. At the conclusion of their mini-concert, they sang one of their most popular songs ever, which ended with the lyrics:

"All you had to do—was to be what you always have wanted to be.
Welcome back—to the love that is in your heart.
Welcome back.
Welcome back.
Welcome back to Jesus!"

The crowd was soaking it up and loving every single second of the concert. Believe me! The band had successfully ushered in the tangible presence of God into our midst—which is the absolute goal of worship. It was another very special night. One for the books!

In fact, one man did write a book about it. His name is Mike MacIntosh, and Billy Graham even wrote the foreword to his amazing testimony, *For the Love of Mike.* In the book he wrote:

The church sanctuary, designed for 350 persons, was jammed with over a thousand; and what was most amazing, they were all young and casually dressed. Further, they were singing their hearts out and lifting their hands in the air.

Something's wrong here, he thought. *Church people don't look like this. Where are the white shirts, the conservative suits, the bow ties, and wing-tip shoes? Where are the girls with white gloves and ribbons in their hair? Where are the old people? The robed preacher—where is he? And the choir? How come no hymnbooks? This place is wholesome. That's it,*

126

wholesome. The people are young and alive and happy. Not square. They're not embarrassed to be here, not embarrassed about Jesus.

Love Song finished their concert, were enthusiastically applauded, and left the stage with their instruments. Their place was taken by a long-haired, bearded man wearing a hippie-style shirt and jeans and carrying a Bible. He couldn't have been more than twenty-one years old. This was Lonnie Frisbee, a hippie who had come to Christ in the Haight-Ashbury district of San Francisco and was later befriended by Pastor Chuck Smith. Chuck used the young man's gift of communicating to reach the flower-power generation with the gospel. To Michael the man looked like the paintings of Jesus he had seen, and he conveyed a kind of authority that Michael didn't seem to mind.[45]

Mike goes on to describe how he committed his life to Christ that night when I gave the invitation. He had previously prayed to Jesus as a child but had drifted into a life of rebellion, confusion, drugs, sex, and rock 'n' roll. At twenty-six, he was near the bottom of the barrel—after chasing UFOs, different gurus, and bad LSD trips—and had even been locked up in a mental institution.

However, he didn't mention in his book that he came up to me in the beginning of the church service, saying, "Oh, preacher, the side of my head is blown off!" That's what he said, and he looked exactly like a street person to me. He had a look in his eyes like he was just…*gone.* If you can imagine some guy coming up to you saying that the side of his head was blown off, what would you say back to him? Especially if you were on the platform trying to share Christ to over a thousand people.

I said, "Go sit down over there." I needed to get rid of him so he wouldn't take my train of thought away. I needed to focus to preach that night.

So he went over and sat on the floor in the crowd.

I don't remember exactly what I preached about, but I do remember that in the middle of the service, the Holy Spirit began to move on me with a "word of knowledge," which is one of the nine

127

gifts of the Spirit available to believers. Let me remind you that the gifts of the Spirit are not just for preachers—they are available to *all* believers in every situation.

I said, "The Lord is showing me that someone here is being healed of LSD flashbacks."

I want to mark this: That was the one and only time in twenty-four years of ministry when I ever called out a word of knowledge for somebody being healed of LSD flashbacks!

Almost immediately the young man with "half of his head blown off" jumped up and started yelling, "I've been healed! I've been healed! It's me! I'm the one who's been healed of LSD flashbacks!"

But at the moment, I didn't think so. He was so radical in what he was saying. He was yelling and making a scene. But Mike *was* healed from LSD flashbacks that night. He later went on to start and pastor Horizon Christian Fellowship in San Diego, which has become one of the largest and most solid churches in the United States.

That evening, after he made an adult decision for Christ, Mike MacIntosh came into our Afterglow service and, along with about a hundred other new believers, was baptized with power from on high, the power and anointing to serve. That's what the baptism of the Holy Spirit is all about. Mike wrote about these experiences in detail, which you can read about in his book. What a mighty, mighty God we serve!

We are created to please God, to be in him through his Son, and to bear good fruit as we abide in his loving presence. That's the target. We are the branches; he is the life-giving vine. With the overcoming power of God, we can and will produce good fruit and hit the target.

I want to interject a little negativity to my story at this point, because the truth is the truth. If you choose to go hard after God, there will ultimately be resistance from within and from without. The spiritual powers and principalities of this world will use every underhanded way to discredit you, stop you, and positively destroy you.

Even though I turned to God with all my heart, my life always seemed to generate enormous controversy, heated discussion, and unending spiritual warfare. You will see the pattern increase as my story moves forward. It's like the devil himself has me on a hit list or something. I'm positive he does. I have come to expect it, to anticipate it, and honestly, to try to prepare for the blows. However, being a somewhat overly sensitive, artistic type, I am never fully prepared for the assaults. Like everyone else, I need prayer, friends, and healthy, loving relationships.

In the midst of tremendous victories throughout my life, I have also been hurt really badly—even in the ministry. For example, I hate to say it, but at the height of the revival, my wife and I were on food stamps! The church paid me twenty-five dollars a week, which made us eligible for public assistance. It produced a growing resentment and wound in my life. In addition, my wife felt isolated and left out, as my responsibilities kept me going in a million directions. It caused so much strife between us. I wrestled with conflicting priorities, usually choosing ministry over family.

The enemy very demonically tried to take me down, destroy my marriage, and set me up with false accusations and even entrapment. It all hurt, especially when it came in the form of lies, half-truths, jealousy, and sometimes backstabbings from people I loved and respected. Nevertheless, I desire to rise above the storm, to forgive and be forgiven, and to be totally transparent and honest with you. I want to tell the good, the bad, and the ugly.

It is absolutely amazing to me that God uses broken vessels like me—and you. Thank God for his grace! I have seen many shortcomings in others also, but it is not my goal to drag into public view all of the dirty laundry of the church. At the same time, the Bible itself does not gloss over the failings of even the most glowing heroes of the faith. I simply want to be obedient to the best of my ability as I tell my story. At this late date after twenty-four years of ministry, I have nothing to hide, believe me. So again I sadly admit that I have failed God many times.

How have I failed God? Not necessarily the way people have accused me, but I have failed in the same way that every human fails

God every day. How does everyone fail God every day? They fail in thought, word, and deed—every day. I am not making excuses. I will confess more of my sins and struggles a little later, possibly in too much detail.

However, right now I have been thrilled to highlight a few stories of the absolutely good and lasting fruit that God has produced out of my journey with him. The good makes everything else worth it. The good is what God focuses on. He deals with us, disciplines, prunes, and all of that—but he always looks at the heart. Man looks at the outward appearances. Remember the verse that declares: "As far as the east is from the west, *so* far has he removed our transgressions from us."[46] Praise God, it's really true!

I am so grateful that somehow, by his grace and divine order, God has used my life to help Greg Laurie, Mike MacIntosh, Danny Lehmann, Chuck Girard, Jill Austin, and many, many others to be a success in the kingdom of God. They are some of the lasting fruit that Jesus has produced out of my life. It is one of the highest callings and privileges possible to minister to the ministers of God.

One more scripture for us to inhale: "And we know that all things work together for good to them that love God, to them who are the called according to his purpose."[47]

THIRTEEN

Fort Lauderdale

I WAS THE RULING, reigning, glorified youth director at Calvary Chapel, but my marriage was failing right in front of me. My wife would often challenge me within a group of people and do a Mexican Hat Dance on my emotions. I left Calvary Chapel simply because I was trying to save my marriage. I quit Calvary Chapel of Costa Mesa and followed my new friend and mentor, Bob Mumford, to Florida. Like I said, I had a desperate need for a father figure and a desperate desire to save my marriage.

I met Bob Mumford when he was my Bible professor at Melodyland School of the Bible in Anaheim, California. It was right across the street from Disneyland. While I was ministering full time during the sizzling Jesus People movement, I was, at the same time, led to go deeper into the Word of God. The Bible clearly directs us to "study to show thyself approved unto God, a workman who needeth not to be ashamed, rightly dividing the word of truth."[48]

I prayed about it, and the door opened for me to attend Melodyland. I was instantly touched by my new professor and inspired by the anointing on this man's life and on his words. He was another strong father figure. Bob's depth of character and his knowledge of Scripture deeply affected my life. We developed a strong friendship, which I still value and appreciate very much.

When Bob was moving out of California to start a new ministry and school with four other well-known leaders in the Christian world, he invited me to make a bold move and join him in Florida. He wanted me to take a break from ministry, focus on my marriage, and attend the new Bible school. After much deliberation, my wife and I were off to Fort Lauderdale. Little did I know that this new endeavor would also become "famous" as the center of a major controversy in Christianity around the entire world.

Two months before I moved to Florida, even before I was seriously considering leaving my post at the church, we had an elders' meeting at Calvary Chapel. Chuck Smith told us that Derek Prince, a well-known minister, was a false prophet. He said that Derek Prince was putting too much of an emphasis on deliverance ministry. From my own personal experiences, I knew that that could easily happen. Chuck was adamant about Derek Prince being a false teacher.

Now, after being in the ministry as long as I have, I've come to understand something. When God wants to put an emphasis on a truth that's been lost, possibly because that truth slipped through the believers' fingers, then God will put an overemphasis on the subject for a time to show his people that he's restoring life to a lost revelation. Deliverance from evil and the reality of spiritual warfare needed to have an emphasis back in the seventies.

Of course, when God is renewing revelation, people can detect the emphasis and then overemphasize the subject themselves. It usually comes out excessive because our tendency is to run ahead with an idea. Kathryn Kuhlman summed it up by saying, "An overemphasis on divine reality becomes spiritual error." Demons are definitely real and diabolical but not behind every bush in the front yard or behind every idle thought in our minds. Since then, Derek Prince has apologized for his overemphasis on deliverance, and the subject has come to a sensible balance now in the body of Christ.

But at that particular time, Chuck Smith labeled Derek Prince a wolf. Chuck was right to be concerned about a point of doctrine, but then he made a big leap and emphatically told his staff that Derek Prince was a wolf in our midst. So the next week, having a juicy tidbit from my bishop, I stood up in front of all of Calvary Chapel at the peak of my success, and I ragged on Derek Prince. I called him a false apostle, a wolf in the body of Christ. I called him a false prophet! How dare he defile the teachings of the Lord by saying that demons could possess Christians and on and on!

No credit was given to Derek Prince for the African influence on his teachings, where years and years of being a missionary in Africa had given him extensive experience in the subject and where he discovered that fighting with the "fun-day theologies" of the time didn't really work. He, on the other hand, only went into the battle with practical applications of deliverance. Those applications did work, and he learned most of them while ministering among people who practiced voodoo, witchcraft, and spiritism.

Here's the point of the story: Within two months, the Lord led me by the Holy Spirit to join the team in Florida—a team that included Derek Prince. Now, I loved and adored Bob Mumford, but I hated and despised Derek Prince. Just two short months after I called him a false prophet and a wolf in the body of Christ, the Lord moved us from my post at Calvary Chapel, where I had multitudes of people who basically burned incense at my altar, to Fort Lauderdale.

When we arrived in Florida, the only apartment in Fort Lauderdale that we could find belonged to, as you can probably guess, Derek Prince. We looked, but everything was booked up because it was summer, and that's where the action is during the summer break—Fort Lauderdale and Daytona Beach. Believe me, my wife and I looked all over the whole city, and the only place that was reasonable enough for us to rent was Derek Prince's rental.

So we rented the apartment and started our life in Florida. We had a place to live, but very soon trials and tribulations joined the party. Because I had chosen to leave my ministry in California, all of my finances were cut off. In addition, there was a severe rumor going around in the body of Christ that I was baptizing my converts in the name of Bob Mumford. There were also swelling rumors and lies about what I was practicing and what I believed in my theology. Suddenly all of this was hitting me in an attack like I had never known before in my entire life.

I remember when we used up all of our savings and I was forced to knock on Derek Prince's door on the day that my rent was due. I cried out, "We don't have no money! I don't have the money, Mr. False Prophet! I don't have the money, Mr. Wolf in the body of Christ!"

He looked at me and said, "I *will* make you responsible financially to me, but I will not require it of you now. I will give you a grace period. You can live in my house, and when God provides the money for you, you can pay me as a landlord."

Derek Prince was full of mercy and grace with a kind voice like a loving father. The Lord pointed out to me that he was no wolf. Out of all the ministers I have met—and believe me, I have met thousands of ministers—Derek Prince is one of the most revered, honest, biblically balanced, and gloriously anointed apostles I have ever met in the body of Christ. He became a lifelong friend and mentor to me.

The Lord showed me so graciously how he loves different people who have different ideas and theologies and that conformity to doctrine is not the same as unity in the faith. That's denominationalism, and I believe with all my heart that denominationalism divides the church today! Wake up! Find the mystery in unity, which is that God would never reveal all of his mysteries to one man, group, denomination, or church structure.

In the creed at Calvary Chapel we say that we are not against denominations except when they come to divide the church. Let's practice what we preach. I mean, we have over four hundred denominations represented in the body of Christ. So God does not reveal his whole truth to a puny man or to a deluded denomination of people who think they are bearing all of the revelation. They are more like a cheap cafeteria than a fine restaurant. God gives different appetites to different people. To see one group of people as having it all reminds me of the parable about a group of people who went to heaven. God was showing everyone around. St. Peter whispered to the crowd, "Shhhh! Be quiet! We're passing the Seventh-day Adventist section of heaven, and they think they're the only ones here."

So anyway, one minute I was railing and ragging on Derek Prince, and two months later he was my landlord! Thus began an eventful five-year-plus adventure in Florida. I stepped *completely* down from any ministry position, attended the new school, focused on my marriage, and submitted to my elders. The leaders of the ministry were Bob Mumford, Don Basham, Ern Baxter, Derek

Prince, and Charles Simpson. They initially formed the Holy Spirit Teaching Mission, but soon renamed it Christian Growth Ministries.

However, the ministry of these five men soon became known as the controversial "Shepherding movement." They developed a strict doctrine of submission to spiritual elders, who were termed "shepherds." The movement was also greatly influenced by Juan Carlos Ortiz, my intellectual friend from Argentina who also joined the ministry.

The strict doctrines were built on many of the teachings of Watchman Nee, who was a radical Chinese convert who inspired millions with his books and absolute sacrificial devotion. He planted churches all over China, and in 1952, the atheistic, Communist government put him in prison. He died in prison twenty years later. As he approached death, he wrote on a scrap piece of paper that a Chinese prison guard later found next to his body. The guard gave it to Nee's niece when she came to pick up his few belongings.

The handwritten scrap of paper said:

Christ is the Son of God who died for the redemption of sinners and resurrected after three days. This is the greatest truth in the universe. I die because of my belief in Christ.
—Watchman Nee

So Fort Lauderdale was all good in the beginning. I myself am inspired by Watchman Nee, Jim Elliott, and other martyrs, but beware, my friends: You don't realize you are walking into spiritual error, legalism, and deception at the onset. It creeps up on you little by little. That's what happened with the Shepherding movement. I'm not going to get into all the controversy, because the leaders have basically renounced any unintended errors in their attempts to minister to people. Reams of commentary have already been written on the subject.

If you follow the teachings of Watchman Nee, you will probably become a little legalistic, but that's not his fault either. He was playing out the hand he was dealt in another culture at a different time. We need to stay in tune with the Holy Spirit for our own lives. That's why it is so important to have a personal, living relationship with God and a solid knowledge of his written Word. The Bible is a very supernatural book. It is, in reality, a game plan for ultimate, eternal life with the Holy Spirit as the umpire of our hearts. Follow him!

I enjoyed the Bible school and even took a construction job hauling cement like my stepfather had done most of his non-military life. I was *very* obedient to my elders and completely laid down my public ministry. You have to understand, if my heart were as full of power and personal ambition as some accused, I would *never* have left my position at Calvary Chapel. I had it all back there. I was out of everything in Florida. However, I did have the opportunity to go on several foreign mission trips with teams led by Bob Mumford and others. The Lord kept my missionary passion burning strong during this period of my life. It was foundational for the deeper call of the Great Commission that God was leading me into.

I was also feeling a new emphasis coming on my life and calling. The operative word was **GO!** I had gone on many mission trips with Calvary Chapel "locally, to nearby states, and to the uttermost parts of the world," but I was feeling increased passion for third-world missions and lost souls everywhere. I am intrigued by different cultures, and the Spirit of God captured my heart with a huge burden for homeless, abandoned children around the world in poverty-stricken nations. I also love to travel. God put it all in my DNA.

I remember this one time while we were in the school in Fort Lauderdale, I was getting ready to leave with a major team of ministers for a whole summer of preaching in Scandinavia. I've now had twelve missions to Scandinavia, preaching in Sweden and Denmark, as well as England, Poland, Germany, and many other European countries. But this particular time there seemed to be an especially severe spiritual assault on our lives. Warfare always happens before a mission trip. Those of you who have gone out on short or long-term mission trips, have you noticed that?

We were just getting ready to leave and had purchased our tickets and responded to letters of invitation. The itinerary was all set up. We were going to take land for Jesus…and then I suddenly fell very ill. It felt like an intense flu with every muscle in my body throbbing and aching. It was the most violent sickness that had ever come on me. I can't explain in words how bad I felt. It was like a type of food poisoning and flu combination or something. We were ready to leave, but I was so sick that there was absolutely no way I could have gone on the trip.

The Lord said, "Go have Mumford pray for you."

So there I was, lying in the back seat of our car, being driven over to Bob Mumford's house. My wife was driving, and she hit a train track too fast. It lifted me up off of the back seat and slammed me back down. It completely wiped me out! It was so painful. All I could do was roll on my side and groan. I couldn't believe how sick I was. Bob Mumford came running out with Dick Keyes and another brother, and he took authority over the attack. He demanded that the enemy let me go in the name of Jesus. I was *instantly* healed! I lie not. Let me tell you, the pain totally went away, and I was instantaneously, miraculously healed! Apparently, this was a very strong attack coming at me because we were getting ready to go into major battle on the mission field.

I'll never forget that healing touch that lifted me right back up on my feet. It was like when Jesus went to Peter's house with his gang, and Peter's mother-in-law was taken with a great fever. Jesus stood over her, rebuked the fever, and immediately she "arose, and ministered unto them."[49] So it was with me. Immediately I got up and went to work for Jesus! People often discount divine healing with skepticism, doubt, and unbelief, but when you experience it yourself or personally witness a blind man suddenly get his vision back, then it's a different ballgame.

We had an amazing time of ministry, divine appointments, and life-changing encounters on that trip. There was a significant revival taking Sweden by storm at the time. So many adventures and exploits followed on these mission trips that I wish I had time to tell it all! We did more than just Sweden. We ministered in Poland, Germany, Israel, Africa, and other nations during this period of my life. I cherish the memories, and it's a total blessing for me even now as I somewhat relive events while sharing them with you. I feel the pleasure and joy of the Lord on me!

Fort Lauderdale and the Shepherding movement almost did me in, but the Lord somehow pulled me through, just like he can pull a camel through the eye of a needle when necessary. Remember when Jesus told his disciples that it would be easier for a camel to go through the eye of a needle than for a rich man to enter into heaven?

They asked, "Who then can be saved?"

He answered, "All things are possible with God."

By the grace of God, he was with Connie and me during our entire time in Florida even though the heavy-handed effects of the Shepherding movement took their toll on our lives and on our marriage. It was absolutely one of the most difficult periods of my life. Believe me!

Nevertheless, even the rich have a loving God who is ready and able to grant them eternal life in the kingdom of God through the sacrifice of the Son. He will pull a caravan of camels through the eye of a needle for you. Nothing is impossible for God!

FOURTEEN

The Garden Tomb

I WANT TO share a story about the Garden Tomb in Jerusalem. This was still back in the seventies when my wife and I were living in Florida. We were taking our first trip to Israel. Many still called it Palestine. I was visiting the Garden Tomb around the corner from Calvary and was praying in the tomb when a college-aged man walked in. He apologized that he had disturbed my meditation. As I was coming out of the tomb, the Lord impressed upon me to witness to him.

I said, "What have you come here for?"

And he replied very sternly, "I have come to find God."

I remembered the movie that Pat Boone was in where he played the angel of the Lord at the tomb when they rolled the stone away. He said to the women: "Why seek ye the living among the dead?"

I felt the presence of the Lord on me, and I announced that very same scripture to the young man: "Why seek ye the living among the dead? He is not here, but is risen."[50]

I felt like a shiny Pat Boone angel. When I spoke those words to him, he was converted. He was baptized with the Holy Spirit with the evidence of glossolalia and spoke in an unknown language. He was struck by the power of God!

A text for this is in Acts 10, when the Spirit of the Lord fell on them at Cornelius's house as Peter preached the gospel to heathen Gentiles. "While Peter yet spoke these words, the Holy Spirit fell on those who heard the word, and they all began to speak in tongues."[51] This is what happened to that man at the entrance of the Garden Tomb. I slipped my card with my address in Florida on it in his pocket, because the tour group that I was with was leaving.

Soon after I got home, a letter came to me in Fort Lauderdale. It was from the young man at the Garden Tomb. He said that he had tried the Jehovah's Witnesses and the Mormons. He was exhausting himself in the cults. He shared how he had saved his money for a year and made a pact with death that if he didn't meet God in the Holy City, then he was going to take a bottle of sleeping pills mixed together with a lethal dosage of narcotics. He was suicidal, overwhelmed with life, and figured it was not worth living if "this is all there is." He would give God one last chance at the Garden Tomb in Jerusalem.

The letter went on to say, "What joy when you stepped out," and he repeated the story of me stepping out of the tomb wearing a long, draping, robe-type shirt (I always wore the half robes that would come down like a real long shirt, but they were designed just like robes), with my long beard and long hair way down to my back.

He said, "You stepped out of the Garden Tomb and gave me the message of the angel." He was born again and baptized with the Holy Spirit. Later he joined a Christian club on his campus and started leading people to the Lord.

He told me a little more detail about the day we met. He had been to the Garden Tomb on three occasions the day before, but it was locked on Sunday. He went back to his hotel room in Jerusalem and cried himself to sleep because he was going to commit suicide. He was holding the pills in his hand, saying, "God, if I do not meet you when I go to the tomb, I am going to take my life."

And there at the Garden Tomb, I became a divine messenger like Philip in the New Testament, who was taken out of a happening revival, led completely out of the city he was ministering in, and sent by God to the wilderness in order to witness to *one* person. And that person was the Ethiopian eunuch who was reading Isaiah 53 and did not know what it meant. What a privilege to be a messenger for the Lord! I only wish I could travel like Philip did after he baptized the eunuch in the river. He was instantly beamed to a distant city. Someday we, too, will most surely travel that way!

THERE IS FREEDOM

That Garden Tomb encounter leads me back to the very dark, disturbing, but important subject of suicide. For whatever reason, the Lord often moves quite differently with me, and if you read my stories recorded in this book, I think you'll agree that God has moved in unusual ways.

One time when I was living in Brea, California, I was scheduled to preach at a church in East LA that was pastored by Jim Pageant (I am beaming ahead in time for a short while!). For the record, nothing about East LA is "easy." As I was beginning to preach, I waited in front of the congregation before I received my speaking orders. I needed to feel the need of the people. Instead of preparing my text two weeks ahead of time, I often waited until I stood before the crowd, and then the Lord would give me my text. Pretty risky for public speakers!

To my surprise, I heard God clearly say, "This morning I want you to minister on suicide."

Well, I knew from ancient history that in the fortress of Masada in Israel, the Romans surrounded the Jewish people who had taken refuge on top of an isolated rock plateau hundreds of feet above the Dead Sea. It took a long time for the Romans to build ramps up to Masada to get to them. However, the 960 Jewish rebels decided to practice mass suicide as a people rather than be subjected to death and torture under the hands of the Romans.

So we have an example of suicide even though it's against our morals and against the rules of the church. Here's a group of people—covenant people—who took their own lives. This is not even to be compared to the way the Jim Jones community went out in Guyana.

I started out that morning in East LA by asking, "How many people have had a husband or a wife, or a brother or a sister, a mom or dad, someone in the immediate family—how many of you have experienced a loved one committing suicide?"

In that small congregation of about two hundred, there were fifteen hands raised. Now just stop and think with me for a moment: Here were fifteen people in a little congregation who were immediate blood or marriage relatives of someone who had committed suicide.

I had them stand up. I explained that according to statistics, suicide often repeats itself in the form of a bloodline curse. So if the mother of a fourteen-year-old girl committed suicide before the daughter was able to receive her own mothering instincts, then that fourteen-year-old girl will likely face suicidal thoughts sometime in her life, maybe on hundreds of occasions, when the enemy comes to bring that curse.

So in effect, the "sins of the father" are being visited upon the third and fourth generations. There are very important Scriptural texts to understand bloodline curses.[52] You would think that God in his compassion, love, and mercy would not allow bonded curses to be passed down. But apparently it's true. So I had these fifteen people stand up.

The Lord again clearly spoke to me and said, "I want you to pray a prayer of deliverance from bloodline curses."

In my own family, my youngest uncle was born again and then tried to convert my family. They all mocked, rejected, and made fun of him. For that and probably many other unknown reasons, he, the father of six little children, went into the garage and committed suicide by gassing himself with automobile exhaust fumes. He taped a garden hose to the exhaust pipe, ran the hose into the car, rolled up the window, and asphyxiated himself. So suicide has touched my family also.

As I continued to follow the leading of the Holy Spirit, he was telling me to break the bloodline curses of suicide. This truly was a visitation of God. People got free, but it was incredibly messy. There was a dynamic in the meeting that I had never personally seen myself, although I did cut my teeth on deliverance ministry when I was eighteen years old in the Haight-Ashbury, dealing with Satan worshippers and Rainbow people from deep, dark, ancient cult practices. From the start, God threw me in the briar patch because that's where my ministry was going to be. So when the rabbit said, "Please don't throw me in the briar patch," he was only hoping that he would be.

In the last chapter of Mark, when Jesus was ascending into heaven, he said, "And these signs shall follow them that believe; In my name shall they cast out devils."[53] The first thing that will bring on a power encounter is to recognize the enemy and have the faith to rise up in your priestly ministry and take authority over the demonic realm. And there it is. He is saying, "You shall cast out demons as a sign that you belong to me."

I want to remind you that many Christians don't acknowledge the devil as a reality, as a personality. They want to pretend that there's some kind of yin-yang concept operating, like Willy Nelson's *"just a little old-fashioned karma coming down."*[54] Yeah, Willy! We've all seen that Willy Nelson has had some good old-fashioned karma come down on him! You can go ahead and yin-yang it if you want and see where that gets you. C. S. Lewis says there are two kinds of Christians the devil loves: ones who are overly fascinated with the things of darkness and ones who do not believe in his existence at all.

I want to emphasize that the Bible clearly says that we *will* deal with dark entities, powers, principalities, and dominions that are not of this world, cosmic powers that rule in the heavens. Read the Book of Job and see how Satan has access to heaven and earth.

So keeping in mind the ignorance in the body of Christ, I will tell you that fifteen of those people started radically shaking in major deliverance. Let me also explain to you that we are to "fall on the Rock." Fall on Jesus, who is the Rock. I boldly say to people who are bound in dysfunctional families or have been captured by addictive, abusive, codependent relationships and been bound to habits and don't know why: **There is freedom for you!** But there *is* a battle, and many people don't want to go through that battle.

These people in East LA were rocking and rolling in deliverance, and I had never seen that happen before to that degree. They started to radically shake, and many of them started to vomit. People were having seizures on the floor, with their hands buckling up and drawing in and with hideous looks on their faces. They were huffing and puffing, hyperventilating, and vomiting. Only God knows the extent of their deliverance and freedom, but it was divinely ordained, and I believe in freedom for each and every one of them.

But sadly, only four days later my roommate committed suicide. His name was Glen. My wife and I had met him in juvenile hall. I had been doing juvenile hall services for a year, ministering to two hundred Protestants and Catholics in the Protestants' service. Then one day the Catholics came to me and asked, "Please will you do our meetings also? You're drawing all of the Catholics into your meetings." So I also ministered to two hundred Catholic and Protestant people in the juvenile hall services for the Catholics. I would preach the message, and the priest would serve them Catholic Communion.

Glen was fifteen years old when he came to my meeting. He was an orphan and had been in eight foster homes. He was born again at fifteen but took his life at twenty-seven. He shot himself in the stomach with my uncle's gun that I had in my home. I could see then that a spirit of suicide could suddenly come and attach itself to an individual. It was so heartbreaking and shocking!

We must break through to "family" in Jesus Christ even though you might have come from a dysfunctional family in your background. The true family of God is not dysfunctional—if we can but enter in. God is my Father, Jesus is my brother, and the precious Holy Spirit is my guide! Dear God, help us, and please receive Glen into your merciful arms. You have shown me, Lord, that suicide is **not** the unforgivable sin!

It became real clear to me that because I chose to minister against the subject, spirits of suicide attacked my camp. They didn't get me, because I want to live. But they got the person who was closest to me at that particular time, a spiritual son in the faith. I saw right then how the devil deals with people. He deceivingly says, like Clint Eastwood in a western, chewing on a toothpick, "You leave me alone, and I'll leave you alone." But that's a lie. Don't believe that. You cannot make peace with your enemy. You have to declare war, not try to make peace, because the devil is a liar. He's a thief, and he comes to steal and destroy. Like I've said many times to people, "The devil shoots *real* bullets!" And he is the accuser of the brethren. Resist in the name of Jesus, and he will flee.

SHARKIE

A final story on the subject. I know this is not light and fluffy. Nevertheless, it is real-world stuff that touches our lives. I was living in the heart of Santa Ana in a home I had inherited, and in that particular neighborhood it was about 5 percent WASP. I was in a ghetto. Down the street was a woman who dealt heroin to the community. One morning I noticed two men outside with hairnets on. (Why are old ladies and Mexicans the only ones who wear hairnets? I don't see any correlation between them. But if I ever needed to figure out what to get my neighbors for a present, it would have been a box of hairnets.) Anyway, one morning I was looking out my window, and two guys with hairnets on were raking my front lawn.

I opened up the window and said, "To what do I owe this privilege for your little gardening trip here this morning, brethren?"

Here was this skinny little preacher challenging two rough-looking Mexicans with Pendletons on, tan khakis that went down to the ground and completely covered their shoes, and with tattoos of skulls everywhere. They were bad, with teardrop tattoos under their eyes.

"Oh no, I spot two teardrops. What does that mean?"

It means they spent time in prison or even killed someone. One teardrop is a warning. If you're real bad, you get two teardrops, and one dude in my front lawn had two teardrops.

I said to them, "Why are you raking my lawn?"

They said, "We're trying to find a gold chain."

Later that morning another group of people were in my yard on their hands and knees. Just out of curiosity, I asked them the same question. They said they were looking for a silver ring. So one group was looking for a gold chain, and the other group was looking for a silver ring. Because there were two different stories, I figured they were lying. Actually, what they had dropped in my yard was a bag of heroin.

I said, "Okay, which is it? Is it a silver ring or a gold chain? Because if I don't find a ring or a chain, I'm not giving back to you what I find."

They said, "It's some stuff."

I didn't run into the kitchen and call the Santa Ana police department. I told them my name was Lonnie, and we made friends.

So one day I was across the street sitting with my young neighbor named Sharkie. He also was dealing hardcore heroin. To those people who have never seen that dark underground world, I'll tell you who walked up to score: high school kids, college students, lawyers, secretaries, bodybuilders. There was such a variety of people and a cross pollination of all types showing up with an addiction to heroin. Normal-looking people, people who functioned well in society, were shooting up.

Sharkie had needle marks, along with tattoos, all up and down his arms. One needle mark after another, and some of those injections had infected. These were nasty-looking infections from dirty needles on his arm. He was twenty-one years old and had a heroin addiction that cost 150 dollars a day. In addition, he just discovered that he got his girlfriend pregnant. He was just a boy himself.

I told Sharkie, "The only deliverance from heroin that I have seen is by getting your life right with the Master, getting born again, and asking Christ to come into your life and to forgive all of your mistakes, failures, and sins."

I could see Sharkie's eyes light up. He asked me if I wanted some hot tea. We sat there on the porch, and I witnessed to him about Christ while heroin addicts strolled up the sidewalk to his house. He had heroin and sold it right there in the open. It became something so slick and streetwise. The exchange couldn't have been noticed by anybody. That's why they called him Sharkie—he was definitely slick.

We sat there, and I shared the Lord with him as we drank our tea. I told him that the strongest bondages that I had ever seen rest on people were heroin addiction and homosexuality, two very strong spirits that are almost impossible to break except for the resurrection power of Jesus Christ.

The very next day, I was watching Donahue talk about how to deal with people who have lost loved ones to suicide. That was the theme of the program. And then I heard this bloody scream. I looked out the window. Sharkie's girlfriend was jumping up and down in the street, running around in a circle, freaking out. She was screaming, "Sharkie killed himself! Sharkie killed himself!"

I ran across the street into his house. Sharkie was hanging on a door in his boxer shorts. He had hanged himself with a brown extension cord from the top of the closet door. He tied the cord to the handle, looped it over the door, and fell on a hangman's noose. His tongue had turned purple and was sticking out of his mouth. His body was still warm. His eyes were open, looking straight ahead. It was so difficult to believe that he was dead. He left a suicide note to God, his mother, and his girlfriend.

Almost immediately I went to see a movie to escape reality. It was *An Officer and a Gentleman*. In the film Richard Gere played a character whose friend also hanged himself in the bathroom. *What is this?* It seemed like I couldn't get away from suicide. It is such a shock to the spirit to be around a dead person who has just taken their life all because they couldn't find happiness.

Suicide has been an unwanted part of my ministry. I believe that you have to be firm with people who are suicidal, but I would strongly advise against trying to handle it personally. When you come to a person who you're sensing all of the indications of depression, withdrawal, and anxiety from, and all the "right" things (which are really the *wrong* things) are coming out of their mouth—seek out some professional counseling.

If everyone could only realize that we don't listen today as a people. We don't listen to our children. We don't listen to our teenagers. Teenagers don't listen to adults. There's such a wide gap between the generations, and it's getting wider. I would advise not to attempt to be a Mr. Fix-It with a messiah complex. However, I think that you should definitely intervene if you see a loved one with indications of suicide. Help them get some professional counseling and spiritual deliverance.

It's a recent phenomenon that suicide is now occurring among nine and ten-year-olds. It has been on the news lately. They've been committing suicide in pacts, where one does it and then five more do it, or they'll do it as a group. This is now happening in the suburbs of middle-class America. Suicide is like a vial of evil poured out upon the earth by some dark angel. We are seeing all kinds of curses, pestilences, and evil being cast upon the people.

We murder our babies like the ancient heathens did, placing their firstborn babies into the hands of Baal, in the red-hot burning hands of a stone idol. We dedicate our lifestyles to Molech and Baal, except in our case, we're skidding into a new twenty-first century. We sacrifice millions of our firstborn on the altars of the abortion clinics. And then the ones we want to keep are killing themselves, and we don't know why. Wake up! We need God more than ever!

In my experience among church people, I found that those with the most success over the devil are the fearless ethnic Pentecostals, the kind who might have a storefront mission down in Coney Island in New York City. They are Christians who do not let the devil threaten them. They have seen too much. No group is perfect, but we need to exercise our spiritual authority in the name of Jesus Christ over the wickedness that assaults us from so many directions. There is deliverance, freedom, and an abundant life in Christ, but we need to enter in and allow God to rescue us. We need to pay attention and not drop our guard by chasing the American Dream.

YOUR COVER STORY

It is 1991 as I write this. In this new decade that we just entered, I feel that God is going to shed a lot of light about supernatural evil beings. Just this week, the headline of *Time* magazine was: "Does it exist—or do bad things just happen?" The rest of the cover was *completely* dark except for the word *EVIL*, written in large black letters. Quite clever the way that they did it. "Is there really evil?"

Back in 1971, *Time* magazine came to our church to do an article. The reporters/photographers Jack and Betty Cheetham had previously covered a major *Look* magazine article with me in it. The same couple was hired by *Time* as free agents to do another article on the Jesus movement (see the story "The Jesus Movement Goes Mainstream" by Jack Cheetham on page 189 in the appendix).

One night in one of our Bible studies, the reporters were divinely struck, and both of them, husband and wife, were born again with tears and repentance. They said they were so thankful that God had broken a major international story for *Look* magazine. They wept, saying it was the greatest opportunity as reporters they had ever had.

Book cover photo by Jack Cheetham

Just think, they were completely lost heathens and never had any idea or any kind of clue at all that you could have a personal relationship with Christ. Their concept of Christianity had been totally distorted by dead religion and the lies of the powers and principalities that influence the airways of the secular world. Darkness does exist, but thank God, Jesus is the light of the world.

The Garden Tomb is empty "for he is risen!" My suicidal friend in Jerusalem found God at the exact spot where God defeated our very last enemy—death. "**O death, where is thy sting? O grave, where is thy victory?**"[55]

Allow God to rescue you from every enemy—including yourself! Back in 1971, everything changed in a moment of time for Jack and Betty Cheetham. That's how fast everything can change with Christ on the cover of your story.

FIFTEEN

Three Nuns in a Chapel

DURING THIS SEASON of my life in the mid to late seventies, I went on another major mission trip to several countries in Europe. This particular trip made a huge impact on my life and future ministry. Two weeks after Pope John Paul II was nominated, we visited a few of his churches in Poland where he had authority. As we went into one of the pope's churches, it was all nicely decorated with flowers and ribbons—Polish style. It was a high celebration with a lot of flowers everywhere at the altar. We heard the people singing softly in the background, "Come to the water*ski*," which was our song.

When we met those people in Poland, they were obviously very committed to God, and they hated Communism. They were definitely Spirit-filled believers. After they sang "Alleluia" and "Come to the Water," they all broke into beautiful glossolalia and worshipped in the Spirit. It was a Spirit-filled Catholic congregation. What a blessing! There was such a presence of God.

We also met friends of the pope back when he was just a local priest. We had long conversations with them. They were shocked that he had been nominated to be the pope. He was the first Polish, non-Italian pope in hundreds of years since there was a Dutch pope in 1523.

We went to Czestochowa, Poland, to a church where they have the famous Black Madonna. It is a national icon and Poland's holiest relic. Legend claims that it is painted on a wooden tabletop from the actual home of Joseph and Mary. The church is actually a quite small chapel. I remember going in and seeing the Black Madonna for the first time. Being an artist, I'm interested in old art. We were invited to be guest speakers at that church and several other churches. I was around fully habited, old-fashioned nuns who only showed their partially framed-in faces.

151

The hotel where we were staying was in Warsaw. My friend and I happened to meet a Polish girl in the lounge, which was kind of a bar, and she was "coming on" to my partner, a married man with five daughters. She was flirting with him, and he was flirting with her. He wanted to lead her to Christ, and she wanted him to be her lover. It was that obvious to me. My friend's intentions were pure, but it can be very dangerous being away from your family and also ministering to attractive single women. You have to be very careful when you're not in the right place. She started coming to our speaking engagements and following us. She turned up wherever we were going for the next part of the program.

When we ministered in Poland, those people were hungry for God. They had been oppressed for so long and wanted to communicate with people who were free and loved the Lord. Poland left a permanent impression on me. I wish that a lot of missionaries would go to Poland, because I believe that the power of God is there to bring in a great harvest. The Lord said, "Say not ye, 'There are yet four months, and *then* cometh the harvest.'? Behold, I say unto you, Lift up your eyes, and look on the fields; for they are white **already** to harvest!"[56] It's true in Poland, and it's true right here in our own backyard.

The time came to minister in the church where the ancient Madonna painting was located. We started praying before the meeting. Then the girl, our new attractive friend from Warsaw, came into the chapel early to be with us. As we continued to pray, an evil spirit apprehended this girl, and she turned into a hideous she-creature. She started to make these awful, shrill sounds. Her face became distorted as if it were being eclipsed by something from the pit. It was terrifying what she was doing—and violent.

I remember going, "Oh my God," and then she went backwards, arched her back, and hit the floor. She was manifesting demonic powers. She was completely and totally possessed by the devil! I had seen this kind of thing before, but even now it is always totally shocking when it's the real deal. I looked around the chapel, and there were three nuns at the altar rails praying in full habits. They had been quietly praying even before the girl arrived. When they heard the demonic manifestations and commotion, they all looked over at us.

The girl screeched out at them, "Waaugh!" like something you would read about in the New Testament. It was classic and happened exactly like this (picture this in your mind): All three nuns turned their heads to the left, in unison, saw what was going on, then immediately turned their heads, *in unison*, back to the altar, and continued to pray even *harder!*

Then that young woman began to wrestle with the presence of the Lord as those Catholic nuns began to intercede in the Spirit! They were definitely Spirit-filled! I was so impressed and thankful! The nuns were on the right-hand side of the chapel (I feel the Holy Spirit all over my whole body even just telling the story). Those precious nuns turned, took one look, and then never looked back after that, because they didn't want to be rude. They just started to pray away! In a short time, the back of that demon was broken, and it came out of her.

But then another one manifested, and we cast that one out too. Each time, there was a separate fight with the entities who possessed that girl. Finally, after every one of those dark spirits came out of her, she was filled with the Holy Ghost. The nuns were absolutely delighted! They thought that was the most fun they'd had since they were ordained! It was a big show in a small chapel!

If it hadn't been for those nuns, we'd have definitely had our hands full. It was serious. There were way too many believers praying in faith against those dark powers who wanted to keep their victim in bondage. That woman got *gloriously* saved with repentance and apologies. It was wonderful! The instant the last demon came out of her, she received Christ, broke through to the baptism of the Holy Spirit, and spoke in tongues. This was not unusual with these Polish Christians. These Catholic Christians sang in the Spirit over there, and it was glorious.

There is a spiritual level that the Polish believers walk in that is very precious. I felt it right away. Outsiders might not understand, but it is because of the terrible persecutions that the people have endured over a very long period of time. If you want to know about suffering, heartbreak, persecution, mass murder, and unbelievable human misery, look at Polish history. It is mind-boggling to look at World War II, the Nazi occupation, and then the iron rule of the Soviet-dominated People's Republic after the war. They estimate that over three million Polish Jews were killed in the war and six million Poles all together. The Communist masters continued the massacre after the war. It is unbelievable what the people have endured. There are documentaries that will take your breath away about the destruction of Warsaw, the invasion of Poland, and the extermination and murder of millions of people. To see what one human can do to another can make you ashamed of belonging to the human race. But thank God for a remnant people who have survived in Poland, who love the Lord with all their hearts! We should take lessons from them.

EAST GERMANY

While we were in Europe, we also went to Berlin. We were with a team and went across the border into East Germany. I was surprised the Communists let us go over the border. It didn't take very long to cross over, but getting back took us two hours. We had to fill out visa papers, etc. It was a long, hard, painful process. Seeing the Berlin Wall brought up a lot of emotions, realizing that people had died trying to cross that border. They died because they didn't want to be held in non-reality.

And talk about non-reality: When I was in East Germany, all of the beautiful churches that had been bombed during the war were not allowed to be rebuilt. Bombed-out cathedrals were everywhere. The bricks were dripping down over the altars. There was dirt and debris covering everything. The stained-glass windows were blown out. Each church was in total ruins. Let me put my emotion on this––it was *shocking*, to say the least. The East German economy was also in ruins after more than thirty years of a Communist dictatorship. Everyone looked like they were in a 1940s movie. The cars were old and outdated. We had to stand in line for things like toilet paper and chickens.

The people were similar to Bulgarians—afraid to talk to strangers. The secret police were about. This one pastor (I spoke at his underground church) had been thrown in jail and beaten many times. They tried to make him deny his faith and become an informer. They made false accusations against him. He had been in prison. The previous pastor of his church had been shot to death at the pulpit.

For the first time, I was able to bask in the wonderful love of the persecuted church behind the Iron Curtain in the seventies. These East German Christians were filled with Jesus because of the persecution, and I will never forget the kind of endurance it produced in the saints there in Eastern Europe. In the church where the pastor was shot to death, they graciously gave us the right hand of fellowship. They wept as we shared. When those Christians went to church, they wept with JOY. They were so grateful to have us come and share even though it was dangerous, and they asked for the prayers of the saints in America.

The whole idea for us about Germany was that we were able to see the endurance they received from the persecution. It made my adrenaline flow as we met with the secret contacts who were bringing us to the meetings. The elder I was traveling with had done it before. We were also smuggling Bibles. Not very many (we weren't Brother Andrew), but we did smuggle as many Bibles as we could to the people. I can honestly say that I smuggled Bibles behind the Iron Curtain, because I did. It was fun, and I enjoyed it. How fantastic an opportunity that was for a young evangelist!

As I mentioned previously, it is 1991 as I write this account. I'm so grateful that the Berlin Wall finally came down. To put a topping on this, God allowed me to be in Germany the day it came down about three years ago. I was pretty tired on that particular trip because I had a long forty-hour journey all together. I was going to South Africa and decided that I needed a rest between my plane rides. So I got a hotel, turned on the TV, got in bed, and witnessed throngs of jubilant people start to tear down the Berlin Wall. I was gloriously rejoicing with the Germans—and the world—that such a strong deception over so many people was coming down! I saw the wall torn down on television while I was actually in Berlin. That was exciting!

The Eastern Bloc Christians were very fascinating. Poland and East Germany in particular challenged me and focused my faith. What a coincidence that a "Christian" nation like America has the most freedom, prosperity, and opportunity for its citizens in the history of mankind, while Communists, Socialists, and dictators of every persuasion more or less enslave their people. A few live in luxury, while millions are imprisoned by powerful deceptions. It is all designed to keep people away from Christ. The danger here in America is that total freedom develops lazy attitudes. Our freedom can be taken for granted and make us complacent and uninformed about what is really going on in the rest of the world. It can make us blind to what is going on spiritually.

Our nation has in many ways turned it's back on God and on our Christian foundation. We are in danger of losing those hard-won freedoms. We need another Jesus People Revival that will turn America and the whole world back to the true King of Kings and Lord of Lords. Remember, all you proud powermongers out there: Someday soon "**every knee *will* bow and every tongue confess that Jesus Christ is Lord!**"[57]

"It is written"—and you can bank on it!

SIXTEEN

"Russia Good!"

ON ONE OF our trips to Africa, we were emphatically warned that Nigeria was very dangerous at that particular time. Nevertheless, we were on our way. In all of my previous missionary experiences, I never had to deal with an aggression in people so hateful to whites. I was accustomed to South Africa, where the black Africans were basically passive to the whites.

When we arrived in Nigeria, it was another story completely. The people were overly aggressive. They cheated you in the stores. They would charge ridiculous amounts of money for basic things. They would lie even in the post office. One time a woman blatantly tried to cheat me when I tried to buy stamps. She was demanding about three times the correct amount of money. I put the stamps in front of her along with my money, but when she tried to cheat me, I took the money back and gave her back the stamps.

In addition to thievery, there's a lot of murder in Nigeria. It's definitely a dangerous country. We were staying in a missionary compound with a twenty-foot wire fence all around it. When you see a huge wire fence surrounding a place, it definitely makes a statement. It was like a little prison to keep people *out*. It even looked like a jail. In Nigeria during the seventies, it was common for people to break in at night to rob and kill. There was just so much extreme poverty and so many people.

We arrived around Christmas. Our team had just been in Poland, where it was freezing cold, and then suddenly we were in Nigeria, which is close to the equator. The first night, there was no hotel available, so we slept on church benches. It was absolutely miserable. One night they arranged for me to be in a room with several other men. I tried to sleep while mosquitos bit me about five hundred times all over my body. It took me almost two weeks to recover from the bites.

We were in a malaria-infested area and had to take malaria pills because the mosquitoes carried the disease. There were rats the size of cats walking around the streets with the people. I lie not. There would be a house with a field next to it, and trash would be as high as a two-story house in the empty field. Then there would be another house and a field, then another house and a field, all littered with mountains of refuse. There was so much trash in Nigeria that it was unbelievable. There was no trash order. People just threw their garbage out in the fields. I was shocked to see it piled up as high as the houses. People lived among the garbage and the rats.

One day as we traveled around the country, we were walking around in a promenade of people. People were everywhere all around us, hundreds of them walking back and forth. I noticed one guy in the crowd had pulled down his pants and proceeded to go to the bathroom right there in front of everyone.

I said to our missionary host, "How come that grown man has pulled down his pants and is defecating right there in front of us?"

The Nigerian guide said, "I don't see what you're talking about."

I pointed directly at the squatting man and asked again, "How come that person is going to the bathroom?"

Our guide said, "Where? What guy? I don't see anybody."

It is the culture not to look. He explained to me, "That is his spot, his private space alone." It wasn't anyone's right to look in on it. I discovered that everyone in Nigeria felt the same way. There were literally multitudes of people in the streets with no toilets or plumbing. Men, women, and children—thousands and thousands of people everywhere. Horrible conditions were completely surrounding us. It was absolutely the filthiest thing I had ever seen in my life. That's one of the things you have to put up with when you go on the mission field to third-world countries: the crud and filth and huge rats the size of family pets.

Like I mentioned, Nigeria was a brand-new experience for me. There came a point on the trip when I wanted to spend some quiet time with the Lord away from my team and do a little exploring at the same time. Even though many strong warnings were given to all of us, I was compelled to leave the compound and go meet the

Nigerians so I could witness for Christ. I met some pretty "heavy" people. One night I was taking a walk, just getting outside the fence for a break. Our host had continued to warn me, but I was too "bright-eyed and bushy-tailed." I wanted some action…and I got it all right.

I turned at an upcoming corner and walked two blocks down from the compound. I ran into a nineteen-year-old Nigerian who spoke pidgin English. I struck up a conversation and made friends with him. He was very pleasant. Little did I know that he was a helper to some Russians who were in the country. They had this little outpost of the Russian army in Nigeria because of the oil fields. Apparently, Russia had a stake in the oil there. Pretty soon one of the Russians happened to come out of his nearby army compound. The place didn't really look like anything military. He was just standing there right by us then came over and talked to me. He also spoke a bit of English. I didn't know he was Russian. I wasn't expecting to meet Russians in Nigeria.

As we were talking, he said, "California. I know California. It's part of United States."

I didn't realize that he and his five fellow soldiers were suspicious of me. Maybe he thought I was a "Yankee capitalist" American spy. My experience in Nigeria was quickly becoming like the movie *The Hunt for Red October*. Then my worst nightmare happened. They invited me into the complex, their compound. It was a Russian army barracks with six soldiers who had been away from Russia for six months. There was obviously an excitement when I came into the compound, because here was an American in a Russian compound in the seventies. The other soldiers came in one at a time. My host had gone into other parts of the pretty big compound and brought them all in to see me one by one. I didn't know it then, but I was their prisoner. For quite a while, I did not realize I was their captive. I was being very nice, trying to represent the Lord.

It was nine o'clock when I left our missionary compound. When I finally tried to leave to go back, the Russian guy in charge locked all the doors, laughed out loud with a hearty Russian laugh, put the key in his top pocket, and looked straight at me.

I said to myself, "Sweet mother of God."

I was terrified, absolutely terrified because they took me as a prisoner. That's really the truth. I've always wanted to tell this Russian story because the partner who I traveled with thought that I went out sinning that night. But I was in the jungles of Nigeria. There was no place to go. I walked two blocks and got captured. They locked me in. I was really concerned that I wasn't going to show back up at our compound. However, my Russian experience in Africa was only beginning. They decided to have me for dinner. I thought they were actually going to eat *me* for dinner! I felt like Friday from *Robinson Crusoe* among the cannibals.

One of the soldiers went to the refrigerator and took out a cold roast duck. They slapped it on the table. They slapped everything down—loud. They took a white block of something and slapped it down. The soldiers slapped the glasses down. One glass, two glasses, three glasses—*bang, bang, bang, bang*—until everyone had a glass. It was all Russian actions, loud and slamming.

Then they said, "Russia good!"

And I said, "America pretty good. I like America."

Here I was, this little long-haired guy up against six wooly-bully Russians, and they were all square and all different ranks in the Russian army. When I realized that I was their "guest" (under lock and key), I decided to forget that I was in danger and to play along and be pleasant. I did my best to go with their program.

They were obviously confused about me. I told them that I was not a spy, that I was not going to cause them any trouble. Nevertheless, when I tried to get away, they wouldn't let me go. The nineteen-year-old Nigerian who spoke pidgin English came back with a large Coke bottle filled with homemade tequila from a cactus there in Nigeria. It was thick and syrupy. When I put ice cubes in it, it did like anisette and turned almost gray. It burned hot all the way down my throat.

The soldiers poured glasses for everyone, and I realized they wanted me to have a drinking contest with them. It was to be America versus Russia. They hit their fists on the table and screamed that Russia was good. I took a deep breath and said that

160

America was also a wonderful place, because I had to drum up my loyalty for my country. That's what was happening—they wanted to see how much I loved my country, so I spoke up.

But it was just me against six Russians. They poured drinking glasses full to the top with this drink from hell. I was terrified not to accept their hospitality, even though I do not consider myself to be a drinker. In my whole life I never participated in anything like I did that night when they forced me to drink with them. And they did, too—force me. I was completely petrified. They put my glass in my hand, put it up to my lips, and were absolutely insisting that I drink with them. I can't fully express how terrified I really was. I had good reason to be. On top of everything, I was super concerned that I had disappeared from my missionary compound with no explanation. What a disaster this was becoming.

The competition between America and Russia was now full on. We drank our first glass of home brew. I must admit that I began to notice things about these soldiers. They were lonely, absolutely lonely. They were desperate. They had been six months away from their families and stuck in the jungles of Nigeria with one another. They couldn't stand each other's guts. I could tell right away. The only focus they had together was *me*, something new and interesting. They were just playing, and after a while, actually started to be friendlier. Every single one of them wanted to show me pictures of their families.

I followed them around the big compound to see their pictures, which they kept in their rooms. Then several of them started to get out their Russian pornography. These were not X-rated photos of people having sex. They were really old pictures of naked Russian women with big hairy armpits. They almost looked like men. I had never seen so much hair on a woman. I could have gone my whole life and not seen those pictures. This all started in after we had our first round.

The drinking contest seemed to be almost like a Russian ceremony or something. They cut squares out of a slab of solid white lard and made me eat it. Of course, if you have tasted lard, you know the feeling that it puts in your mouth. It coats the whole lining of your taste buds in your mouth. It was just like sucking on whale blubber. I had to eat a square of lard, but I didn't know why. I found out later it was to line the stomach so that I could drink a ton of alcohol. The lard would allow all of us to get insanely drunk but not so drunk that we'd pass out.

So I was forced to eat my first block of lard, not knowing what it was going to do to me. It absolutely made me sick. We immediately chased the lard down with more homemade "white lightning" while these bully Russians kept screaming about how good Russia was. They provoked me to put up a good show for America. I did my best. Out of terror and incarceration, I sacrificed what I normally would have never gone along with: I became a passive guest. I suggest passivity in some dangerous situations but then not in others.

Soon they proceeded to eat their dinner with me. They put the roast duck on the table. They slammed it down with a couple of other things, picked up a chair, and slammed that down. They were slapping and slamming everything around like they do in a Russian dance—*Hey!*—and then they picked me up and slammed my skinny little ass into the chair. They did! Two of them physically picked me up by my elbows and arms and slammed me down into the seat. I was going, "God, help me!" I did not know what was going to happen. So then we ate dinner together. Pretty soon the boy came back and had two more bottles with him. Now it was already going on one o'clock in the morning. I was so concerned.

The soldiers poured more drinks, cut more lard, and made me eat another chunk. We drank another round, and then they cut more lard. We drank another round, and of course, I began to falter in this drinking contest because I'm not a drinker. I dropped acid in junior high school, but I never even drank a beer until I was twenty-five years old. I was naïve to booze. I just never drank. I even had insurance that said I didn't drink because I was in the ministry.

This highly potent Nigerian drink started to form a bond between the Russians and me. Our drinking was definitely creating a type of camaraderie. I realized for the first time that that's what alcohol does among male companions in any country or civilization. Drinking can be a male-bonding thing!

The next glass I could not drink. I tried, but it wouldn't go down. It *couldn't* go down. I was fake gulping, kind of like Engineer Bill playing Red Light, Green Light. I tried holding up my glass of milk to Engineer Bill, but my drink still wouldn't go down. So I pretended like I was drinking, because they were all watching. We stood, and the battle heated up.

For the millionth time, they slammed their glasses down on the table and shouted, "Russia good!"

Of course, I was spilling my drink and pretending, but not really drinking that much. I drunkenly put my glass down on the table and then sheepishly reminded them again: "America's okay too!"

The Russian soldiers yelled back, "Nooo!"

This happened at the end of every drink, so by this point I was slurring, "America." I want to say that everyone would have been so proud of me. I tried. I was a little boy in that situation. You are hopelessly captive to your child at times.

They screamed at me, then filled their glasses to the top, filled my half-full glass to the top again, and cut me another piece of lard. Right around two o'clock or later, we ran out of booze. Thank God! We drank so much that it actually became very dangerous levels of alcohol. The lard was absorbing the alcohol and coating and protecting my stomach.

One of the drunk Russians wanted to show me something, so I followed him to his quarters. I had told them earlier that I was a missionary, and when we got to his room, this soldier showed me pictures he had of his Lord. He had pictures of Jesus, and he had a Bible. He was a believer. He started to tell me in Russian, since he didn't speak any English at all, that he was a Christian through his mother. We were forced to use sign language and also drawings on paper to communicate. We connected like that for quite a while. It was like we played a game of tipsy charades, but it was obvious that Christ had come into his heart and that he loved Jesus. It was not hard to figure out even though we were totally drunk: "Right on, comrade!" By the way, he was one of the Russians who was forcing me into this escapade, of which I became a "willing" participant. I had no choice. They had taken me captive. I shared Christ with him the best I could. I really was sincerely touched in a foggy, pleasantly surprised sort of way.

Back with his friends, I gave everyone a dollar bill. When I gave them a dollar each, they turned into little Russian boys. They were so glad that I gave them a present from the United States. They had never seen American money. They all were so proud of their dollars, that they started showering Russian money on me, hugging me, and picking me up off the ground with big Russian bear hugs.

Then they put on Russian opera. Everyone was so drunk, and now they were playing Russian opera! It was so bizarre. They decided that I was okay. At three o'clock in the morning, they finally let me go. The door flew open, and we all stumbled out into the street. They were singing Russian songs, slapping each other on their backs—six Russians taking me home. They didn't know where I lived, which was only two blocks around the corner.

I said to the Lord, "Heeeey, Loooord, what am I going to do with six drunk Russians?"

I pictured my missionary team coming out at 3 a.m. to greet us in our condition. So I took off running. I ran, and they thought that something was wrong. They sent the nineteen-year-old Nigerian to chase me. By the way, Nigerians are some of the fastest runners in the world (I found that out). I took twenty-five steps, and he took three. In seconds he was on me. He tackled me, and my face hit the dirt. I was completely covered with Nigerian dirt on my face, in my hair, everything.

I was lying there in the dirt, saying, "Oh well, let's just continue to go along with the show."

He picked me up, forced my hands behind me, and brought me back. The soldiers took me and made me crawl up into the cab of a big Russian military truck. I had to literally crawl up into the huge truck so they could all get in—and drive me two blocks down the road. We were absolutely drunk out of our heads on African tequila.

I was finally back at my compound, but it was all locked up. Every night they locked it. I knocked away and called for them to let me in. Over and over, I banged on the entrance. There was no response, only dead silence on the deserted African street.

164

The Russians felt so sorry for me. Finally, they had to take me back to the Russian barracks. They locked me in a cell with bars on it. I vomited all night long. I feel so sorry for people who are addicted to drinking. It was also horrible because I had all that lard in my stomach. I was so drunk the room was spinning around, and every time I put my head up, I vomited, and it literally hit the wall. Linda Blair in *The Exorcist* had nothing on me. When the soldiers came to get me in the morning, vomit was all over. They weren't upset; they were nice people and just wanted to spend time with me.

That was on a Saturday night, and the next morning I was scheduled to preach in a big church. I woke up in a totally sick, hungover panic. At last, they let me out of the barracks. It was nine o'clock in the morning when I woke up, and I had a meeting in half an hour.

I ran back and told everyone that I had been kidnapped by Russians. Nobody believed me. Nobody! Not one person believed me. I remember my feelings being so hurt. (By the way, later my traveling partner went to important leaders and told them that I was using drugs and committing sin. He "knew" this because of that night that I didn't come home. He completely did me in.) But that morning I had to go preach in this big congregation in Nigeria.

There I was Sunday morning in a 90-degree church with 100 percent humidity. I started sweating alcohol like a pig. I sat there praying, "Oh God, please help me. I'm in this situation. I feel so weak. I feel so rotten. I feel so terrible—like vomit." I couldn't seem to get the smell of the vomit and the alcohol off even after I washed and brushed my teeth. The sickening smell just stayed, and the alcohol came out of my sweat glands all over my body. I smelled like someone who had embraced alcoholism for fifty years.

I sat in that church praying to God in a half-drunk stupor of repentance—then I was able to get up and, under the anointing of the Holy Spirit, speak perfectly. The whole drunken state lifted off of me because of the anointing of the Holy Spirit! Our God is truly incredible!

THE HIGHLIGHT

I'll never forget that night locked up with those soldiers. The Lord showed me the highlight of that "adventure" and what it was really all about. It was about the one Russian. He was a lonely Christian, all alone there. When I found out that he was born again, I was very surprised. He was a secret believer among his comrades and was extremely delighted to be able to share Christ with me. He was totally praising God that I came there, but it was under very hard circumstances. My Russian friend needed help. He had a Russian Bible and pictures of Jesus hidden in his private possessions, while the others had pictures of ugly, naked Russian women.

After Nigeria, we went to Ghana. We spoke to huge crowds of people who had walked fifty miles to hear us. There was glorious singing. We did meetings all the time. That particular trip consisted of Poland, East Germany, Nigeria, Ghana, and Holland. We went back through Holland and stayed in The Hague, preaching at big meetings in that country also. Many, many things happened on these mission trips that would take forever to tell it all, which is why the second part of my life story is about my mission work around the world. I love serving God on the mission field. It's all about the Great Commission:

> Go ye therefore, and teach all nations, baptizing them in the name of the Father, and of the Son, and of the Holy Ghost: Teaching them to observe all things whatsoever I have commanded you: and, lo, I am with you always, even unto the end of the world.[58]

I definitely love it—along with the good, the bad, and even some totally ugly Russians!

SEVENTEEN
California or Bust

OUR TIME IN Fort Lauderdale, Florida, came to an end, and my wife and I drove west across the United States. California was calling our name. I mean, the *Lord* was calling us home. It was bittersweet. There were a lot of complex aspects of our time in Fort Lauderdale and a lot to process. However, in the short run, we had a long journey ahead of us. It's a long, long, long drive from Florida to the Golden State and to the beautiful Pacific Ocean. Even though we had been through some recent trying times, both Connie and I were excited about returning to California. The Lord gave us several interesting experiences on the cross-country trek, and I'd like to share a couple.

Everybody who has been around my ministry has heard about us coming through Texas at about four o'clock in the morning. By the time we reached Texas, we had been pushing hard. And then crossing Texas takes like *forever*. A long drive gives you time to think and reflect. I was thinking about the anointing of God. *You* try and win souls without the anointing, without God's blessing on your life; *you* try to make power encounters without the gift of miracles.

Back then, I was sure that the Lord was calling me to receive Oral Roberts's mantle when he died. I wanted to have the gift of miracles so bad I could just taste it. I have dragged people out of wheelchairs—across platforms in front of thousands of people—and they didn't get healed. I dragged them out of wheelchairs, and they were going, "Nooo!" And I was going, "Yes, you're going to be healed—if it kills ya!" I literally dragged cripples out of wheelchairs. That's how bad I wanted the anointing.

So as we were crossing Texas this one morning, I had four cups of coffee. I had reached "caffeine consciousness." We were at a small café, and there was "my" man with a neck brace on, walking into the men's bathroom. I said to myself, "Ah, I feel in the name of the

Lord that I have that man's healing. As a matter of fact, I'm sure of it!"

I went into the bathroom and said, "Hello, my name's Lonnie Frisbee. I have your healing."

The guy didn't speak any English. He didn't know what I was talking about.

I asked, "Can I pray for you?" I thought he said yes, so I grabbed hold of his head and shouted, "Be thou healed in the name of Jesus!"

He started screaming, "Ahhhhhhhh!" in pain.

I ran out and told Connie, "Quick, honey, get in the car before the police come!"

Like I said, you fail your way into God. You fail your way into the kingdom of God.

Fast-forward many years later: I was in a Baptist church in South Africa with John McClure, Kenn Gulliksen, John Wimber, Tom Stipe, and a large team. Back then we drew lots to determine who was going to preach, and that night it had fallen to me.

When I was on stage, a fifty-seven-year-old blind switchboard operator was led to me on the arm of her friend. The operator said, "I understand that you pray for blind people."

I'm like, "Sure! Every day, lady!"

I looked at the back door and could see the green exit sign. I wanted to run toward the green light because, after all, I was in a Baptist church. You know, they don't believe in divine healing. It doesn't make any difference where you are, if you're Baptist, you're not into that. Well anyway, to make a long story longer, the lady had a deteriorating nerve disease as a young woman. Her sister was also blind from the same disease.

I said, "Look up." I stretched my hands out and said, "Look up in the name of Jesus."

She looked up, opened her eyes, and the Lord restored her sight—instantly! Soon that story went out in an article in the *Sun Times* with a picture of the woman and her Seeing Eye dog. It made the headlines of the local papers in South Africa, and thousands and thousands saw the story.

If I would have prayed for somebody in Santa Ana, California, and that person got healed, it wouldn't have even been in the paper. But in South Africa, it made the headlines. You know what else? That story gave me big meetings. Again I'll say—if you have success in the supernatural, people will beat a path to your door.

THE MURDERER

So back to when Connie and I made our way across Texas. As we drove, we saw a hitchhiker and wanted to have him share in the driving. Now, let me give you a warning here: The Holy Spirit led me to stop for that hitchhiker, but I would never tell anyone to pick up hitchhikers. Today, people should not pick up hitchhikers. It's too dangerous. But because my wife and I were out of the hippy movement, we moved in a kind of "gut feeling to do something" mode. Besides, it was still the seventies, and things were much more simple back then. We passed this hitchhiker and stopped for him. However, he didn't see us pull over on the busy highway, so we kept moving on.

Later as we were leaving a coffee shop, we saw the hitchhiker again. We pulled over a second time to pick him up, and this time he got in the car.

The Holy Spirit said to me, "He's a murderer." He spoke those words clearly to me: "He is a murderer." So that's how the story started to unfold.

We drove along, making good time through New Mexico in my old Lincoln Continental with balloon tires. It was airtight and had a nice stereo. While we were listening to the radio, a Bible preacher came on. It was the old-fashioned kind of preaching from some hard-core radical on a Texas radio station. He was saying things like, "Turn your radio on and get in touch with God! Jesus on the mainline here—call him up, folks!"

When the hitchhiker heard the radio, he started reacting to the preaching of the gospel. He became agitated and made a couple of negative comments.

Then the Holy Spirit said to me, "Tell him that he's a murderer. Tell him that I told you he's a murderer."

Again, not only do I advise against picking up hitchhikers, but on top of that, I *definitely* do not advise anyone to get in over their head with complicated ministry. Nevertheless, because I believe in deliverance ministry—seeing people set free from unclean, foul spirits—I said to him, "When you got in the car, the Lord told me and is telling me right now to tell you that I know you're a murderer."

Well, he totally lost his composure. He began to weep at three o'clock in the morning as we drove through New Mexico. He was totally shocked and slammed by the Holy Spirit. He began to break down and tell me that while he was a platoon leader in Vietnam, he often got really stoned. The whole platoon smoked some heavy marijuana buds flaked out with heroin. When they went out on their maneuvers one day, they took a wrong course on the map, which led them right into the midst of a heavily occupied enemy area. They didn't realize where they were and that they had camped out right next to a large North Vietnamese force.

He told me, "Lonnie, I was drinking a hot, steamy cup of cocoa. The other soldiers were cooking breakfast out of cans and tins. We were all sitting around, still stoned out of our freaking minds, and Viet Cong soldiers came running down a path into our camp. They were able to overrun our position because I had become confused as a leader. I had led my platoon the wrong way, and the enemy was suddenly upon us."

Everyone in his platoon was killed except for him and his best friend. The hitchhiker had a blown eardrum. His friend had his legs severely shot up. They radioed for help, and U.S. forces were able to pull him and his friend out by helicopter, but his best friend lost both his legs. He began to feel extremely guilty because many of these men went through boot camp with him. They were buddies like Billy Joel sang about: *"We'd all go down together."*[59]

He had lost his direction while under the influence of drugs that they were *all* using, but he was the one in authority. He felt responsible for their deaths. This deeply affected him for the rest of his life. He was consumed with hate. Then he began to murder Vietnamese people. This didn't have anything to do with defending our country. He started to eliminate the "enemy" whenever he could. He would just randomly kill people. It became something that he enjoyed. It was attached to a demon of murder.

Later in that long drawn out war, a fifteen-year-old Vietnamese girl shot a weapon into the barracks where this hitchhiker was on guard duty. He lifted up the scope of his rifle and blew her head off. He just lifted up his weapon and blew a fifteen-year-old girl's head off. Then he was court-martialed and subsequently confessed that he was secretly murdering the enemy along the way.

Back in the States, the hitchhiker was prosecuted for war crimes in a trial that ended up costing his father all of the family savings. To make things worse, his alleged crimes were in the aftermath of the Calley war crimes, if you remember those headlines. Lt. William Calley was court-martialed for slaughtering hundreds of innocent women and children in a South Vietnamese village. It was the My Lai Massacre in 1968.

So while I was in the car with this hitchhiker, God gave me a word of knowledge. There was no way I could have known. There was no way that I wanted to know! So right when a full moon was going down over the purple horizon of the New Mexico desert, I pulled over. We got out of the car and got down on our knees. As the sun was coming up, I addressed that spirit of murder. It had overcome the young soldier as a total controlling power. He had been cleverly manipulated into letting that thing come upon him and relieve him, by murder, of his guilt. I shared the whole story of the redemption of Christ and how the Lord redeems people off of the slavery block. The result of being a slave on the slavery block is that you become a slave unto death and sin. I told that demon of murder to get the hell out! It went yipping down the street like a dog struck by a car. It got out because I commanded it in the name of Jesus. That young man was set free, and "if the Son sets you free, you are free indeed!"[60]

SUPERNATURALLY NATURAL

Now, Jesus puts guidelines around this, and I must go over the guidelines. I know I did it somewhat before, but this is extremely important. Scripture declares, "You shall cast out demons as a sign that you believe in me."[61] Jesus also warns, "Do not rejoice that the demons of hell are under your authority or that they are subject to you." The reason he says this goes way out there in a type of a concept, a concept of humility, respect, and obedience. He continues to say, "But rejoice that your names are written in the Book of Life."[62]

If you begin to deal with demons and you don't know what you're doing, it can be big trouble. They're much more clever than you are. They'll trip you up with lies and deception and lead you down a primrose lane. A word of knowledge was the thing that came through here with the hitchhiker. It was and is one of the gifts from the Spirit of God that was operative. We don't walk around putting our index fingers on our forehead when we need that kind of information. You know, like the Amazing Kreskin. That's not the way we move in the Spirit—no! The Lord moves in naturally supernatural ways!

The Lord wants to get these wonderful gifts down into his humble, yielded sons and daughters. It's one of the main themes of my story. If God can use a pretty messed up person like me, he can use anyone who comes to him in faith. He can use you. But we're so scientifically oriented that when anything supernatural begins to occur, we get afraid. It's fear that cancels out faith. Your faith begins to move supernaturally, but then fear raises its ugly head and cancels out faith. Thus, you shoot blanks. But God does not want us to shoot blanks. He wants us to have real ammo because we're fighting a real war.[63]

You cannot defeat—this is so important—you cannot defeat a supernatural enemy without supernatural giftedness! Trust God, dive into his Word, learn of him, walk in the Spirit. He is available and ready to partner with us in every circumstance of life. We're talking about the God of the universe who wants to partner with you in every aspect of your life—eternally!

For instance, Shadrach, Meshach, and Abednego would have burned alive in the furnace if there hadn't been a fourth person in the furnace with them, a fourth person who was "like the Son of God."[64] This fourth person supernaturally delivered them from the red-hot flames. By the way, that was Jesus centuries before he took on human form.

But Shadrach, Meshach, and Abednego said, "We shall not bend to your way, O king."[65] And that was the social way. It was the social structure of King Nebuchadnezzar who had demanded to be worshipped—or else.

God showed up supernaturally twice in that story. It's a beautiful, anointed moment when this all becomes real to you. *He* was with the Hebrew children in the fiery furnace and also when a hand magically appeared to King Nebuchadnezzar and began writing on the wall. The handwriting said, *"Mene, Mene, Tekel, Upharsin,"* which means, "You have been weighed in the balances and come up wanting."[66] God allowed that sovereign to go mad—wearing no clothes and eating grass—for seven years. Instead of that, be like the Hebrew children who would not bend a knee to an egotistical earthly king, no matter what.

DRAW ON THE LORD

We cannot even enter into battle with the enemy and win unless we draw on the Lord: "They that wait upon the Lord shall renew their strength; they shall mount up with wings as eagles; they shall run, and not be weary; and they shall walk, and not faint."[67]

David said, "I shall not be afraid of ten thousand people, that have set themselves against me."[68]

But here's a little warning to the people who choose not to deal with the devil as he tries to destroy your life, family, and ministry. In a hurricane, you take the waves straight on. If you don't go straight into the waves, it will break the boat. It will turn you over. You have to, when being confronted by the powers of darkness, take courage and remember what Elisha said to the Lord concerning his servant, "Open the eyes of my friend."[69] All around them were the armies of the enemy. People who look at the conditions and the circumstances of life cry out, "Oh God!" in terrible fear like Elisha's servant. But the prophet of God said, "Open his eyes and let him see." There were angels encamped around the enemy—thousands and thousands of warrior angels. And when I say, "Take courage," I want you to know that only a third of the angelic host followed after Satan. Thus, we have two faithful warring angels to every dark one. Believe in the supernatural, and know that you are not alone in this battle!

There is a battle, though. Life is definitely full of challenges. No one is immune. Have you ever noticed that? If it's not one thing, it's another. God refines us in the fire. I wish there were an easier way, but the cross was definitely not easy for Jesus. Think about that. "For the joy that was set before him, he endured the cross!"[70]

My wife, Connie, and I were on the road heading west, closing in on California. New opportunities and new storms loomed straight ahead on the horizon. Little did I know how severe those storms would be. Listen, the only thing in life that keeps me going is the Lord. He boldly says, "In this world ye shall have tribulation: **but** be of good cheer; I have overcome the world."[71]

Thank you, Jesus, for the guardian angels that you assign. Thank you for your traveling mercies and for finally getting us safely back to California!

EIGHTEEN

The Cousin's Hand

According to statistics from Fuller Theological Seminary, the Jesus People movement was the largest ingathering of souls in the history of the United States. It overshadowed the Great Awakening. It was such a privilege to have been involved and to see God pour out his love and salvation to so many hurting people. It was absolutely incredible! There were some casualties, though.

After five and a half years in Fort Lauderdale, my wife and I returned to California. To this day, I still love and respect Bob Mumford, Derek Prince, and the other leaders, but the heavy-handed Shepherding experience almost did me in. It *did* do me in in many ways, and it was also a disaster for Connie's and my relationship. I went to Florida to try to save my marriage, but now it was falling apart big time.

Nevertheless, Chuck Smith felt that God wasn't through using me as an evangelist, and he graciously invited me to go back on staff at Calvary Chapel Costa Mesa. What a blessing! What a miracle! It was my second tour of duty with Calvary Chapel, which had grown to an immense size with multiplied thousands of new members, a huge new facility, a fully accredited school, and hundreds of new churches being planted or adopted under their umbrella. I lost count of the Calvary Chapels around the world.

At the home church, Chuck Smith tirelessly preached in three back-to-back services every Sunday morning for decades. It is quite impressive. His solid Bible teaching and style of ministry has been the model for scores of leaders and has reached huge segments of society here in the United States and in many other countries.

However, while I was at the peak of this ministry success, my marriage was destroyed by an adulterous affair. My wife had an affair with a born-again Christian and my personal friend, and they lived in open adultery, in full view of the flock of God we had raised up. I was so devastated that I really didn't want to live. I couldn't eat for weeks. I was more or less a "walking dead man." At church while I was preaching, I would see them together in the crowd. Still, the Lord told me that I must forgive my wife and her lover.

I said to the Lord through tears, "I can't."

Then the Lord was silent. And then he came back to me. The Lord visits me like when he came in the "cool of the day" to speak with Adam.[72] I found myself hiding from the presence of the Lord because I found it impossible to forgive my wife's lover, that person who confessed Christ and went to church with my wife on Sundays while living in adultery. People often think that it's the Ten Suggestions, not the Ten Commandments. She was still married to me, but she lived with this man, a former friend of mine, in my house for one year. The hate built up.

One year after they had been involved in this dirty, disgusting relationship of adultery, I came to my door at about 11 p.m. because I heard a hesitant knock. When I opened the door, my wife's boyfriend stood there. He had discovered her making love with his best friend. He broke down and wept.

He said, "We have something in common. We're in love with the same woman." Then he cried like a baby in my arms.

I discovered a secret in that moment: If we walk with the Lord and discover him above everyone, he will even bring our closest enemies—or let's say our *greatest* enemies—to our feet. The two of us stayed up all night talking about Jesus as if we were two young boys catching up on the things that young men talk about. A special feeling of God's love filled the room.

Then he asked me, "Will you please baptize me?"

So the next morning we went down to the San Lorenzo River in Santa Cruz, and I baptized him. When he came up out of the waters of baptism, the love of God was there to meet him in a special way and—thank you, Father—to soothe my broken heart from the bitterness, jealousy, hatred, and anger that had **consumed** me.

As he came up out of the water, as he came up out of the grave, God truly cleansed his heart and forgave his transgressions and sins against me. God actually bonded us in the love of Jesus Christ. After all, it was exactly what he was looking for. He was trying to find fulfillment. But you are mistaken if you think you can find in a relationship with a woman what only God has to offer in the divine. Or you're beside yourself if you think that a man is gonna fill the empty space that has exclusively been ordained for God.

Ultimately, the Lord said, "Father, forgive them; for they know not what they do."[73] And to me he said, "You answered me correctly, Lonnie, when you admitted that it was impossible for you to forgive this man after he committed such transgressions against the covenant of your marriage. I have already forgiven him on the cross. You cannot forgive him with your own worldly strength—but through my divine forgiveness, I have purchased his redemption."

The Lord reminded me that the sins we let go of are forgiven, but the sins we hold on to and retain over other people shall be held against them. The Lord said, "Love me. Forgive this man through me. I need a vessel of mercy, Lonnie."

So as I gave myself over in reckless abandon, God let my brother come home to the Lord through my ministry. He let me forgive him. It reminds me of Corrie ten Boom when she said that she had a more difficult time forgiving her Christian brethren than she did the Nazi murderers who killed her sister and her father.

Divine love takes the cousin's hand of mercy. And Christ triumphs once again so that no flesh may glory in his presence. David said, "If I ascend into heaven, thou art there; if I make my bed in hell, behold, thou art there."[74] So I met the Lord in one of the deepest valleys of my life, with reconciliation with my brother.

Good story, huh?

NINETEEN

Birgitta

AS I WIND DOWN this portion of my story, I want to mention the story of Jonah in the Bible. It is a supernatural tale that is almost hard to believe, but I believe it. I have had several Jonah experiences in my own life. There is much to learn from this disobedient servant of God who was in the act of fleeing from the call on his life. Most of us have heard since childhood how God had a giant whale swallow Jonah in the sea and changed his direction by 180 degrees. It happened, and it changed a nation. It still can.

Just before Jonah was absorbed by the juices and the acids in the belly of the whale, just before he was about to expire, he said, "**Okay**." Just before he was digested in the monster, he was purged and washed ashore exactly where he was supposed to be. Instead of having to come up with the money for a Pan Am flight to Nineveh, the Lord by divine guidance drove him by the obedient fish, and he was delivered onto the shore nearby where he was supposed to go— *"Yee ha ha!"* It is a wonderful story.

Jonah was covered with whale vomit and seaweed. His skin had obviously been bleached white. He had the pungent odor of fish vomit, as well as a stunned look from being half-blinded by the juices of the fish. He was not only near death but struck by God himself.

So when Jonah yelled, "Hey!" to the city, it was the condition of the prophet, not his words alone, that persuaded the king. Here's a beautiful scripture to back this up: "All things work together for good to them that love God, to them who are the called according to his purpose."[75]

Jonah loved the Lord—but he didn't love Nineveh. He was called according to HIS purposes, and it was the purposes of God that forced him through the valley of the shadow of death, through to the other side of the resurrection, and to the obedience of his will. *Whew!* Heavy, deep, glorious oil! So it was the process of life that

179

birthed Jonah into a prophetic ministry to save a whole nation of people that he personally had absolutely no love for at all.

I will share about my personal call to the Great Commission—to **go** to the uttermost parts of the world—in the second part of my story. It is amazing what the Lord did with such an unlikely candidate as myself. I would soon have my own experiences in the belly of a whale as I tried to escape the calling on my life. I became overwhelmed several times with the battle. It became so intense. However, the Lord chose to use me in yet another major move of God that has caught a lot of attention and touched many thousands of lives. That's a little preview.

When I began to travel all over the world as an evangelist for the second time with Calvary Chapel and Maranatha Music in the late seventies, it was a very special time, but I was still devastated by the failure of my marriage. It was also not all Connie's fault. I need to say that. I know that I definitely am not the easiest person to live with. In the final analysis, I lost my marriage in the ministry—something that is not supposed to happen. It totally knocked the wind out of me, and it took a long while for me to get back up. I was literally on the floor but finally picked myself up by the grace of God and marched forward.

On one particular outreach to Yakima, Washington, a man from Sweden was in charge of the meeting. This man had been a missionary in Bangladesh, where he had contracted mononucleosis and also suffered somewhat of a nervous breakdown. He had been physically healed in one of my meetings in Sweden years before. The Lord also revived him from "missionary burnout" in that same meeting.

When he found out that Lonnie Frisbee was the evangelist traveling with the Maranatha band, however, he absolutely forbade me to preach. It didn't matter that he had been miraculously healed in one of my meetings. It also didn't matter that God had used me to help restore him from burning out as a missionary. Obviously, he related to a camp that had a certain opinion about me. In fact, Bob Mumford had been very upset that I left his ministry, and this man had close ties with Bob's ministry. He point-blank forbade me from preaching. I was truly devastated. Rejection is never easy to embrace for anyone, especially if you were weaned on it.

Here's a picture: It's called "Hang down your head, Tom Dooley." I walked down several very long, totally unfamiliar streets in Washington State, hanging my head, having a real-life pity party. For *hours* I ambled along, emphatically expressing my feelings to the Lord.

I angrily informed God, "I am quitting the ministry. I cannot minister in this *confusion* that exists in the body of Christ! I am going to move my life away from this madness. It is unbelievably hard for me. Thank you—but *no thanks!*"

I did not want to be a minister anymore, because this man refused to let me do my job. He said, "We want the band to sing, but we don't want you." He said that to my face.

After my walk, I entered the home of an assistant pastor who, ironically, had just returned from Stockholm, Sweden. I went into the family room and noticed a book on the coffee table. As I sat down, I picked up the book and casually opened its pages. I definitely needed to focus on something besides my emotions.

It was a book of biblical illustrations, poetry, and Scripture. Now, keep in mind that I had just moments before informed the Lord that I was resigning from the ministry. I opened the illustrated book from Sweden. Naturally, it was completely in Swedish. But then I was suddenly looking at a full-spread, glorious painting of Jesus with his arms stretched out and me, Lonnie Frisbee, speaking into a microphone in the bosom of Christ. Immediately the power of God fell all over me and went completely down to my itty-bitty toes.

The Lord said, "You will never get out of the ministry."

I said, "But what if I'm in sin?"

"Doesn't matter."

"What if I'm in rebellion against you?"

He said, "I still love you anyway. But get this and get this good: You will **never** be out of the ministry, *no matter what!*"

All I can say is that it blew my mind in a wonderful way. It was an outpouring of love from God at a time when I needed it the most.

I felt a healing begin at my very essence as the Lord applied his ax to a root of low self-worth and self-destructiveness. Scripture says that even if our hearts condemn us, God is greater than our hearts.[76] This was my third attempt to desperately relieve myself from the calling of God on my life.

I had made another escape run, but God possesses a "divine bola." That's what Argentine gauchos use to catch their cattle. It's two stones wrapped in soft leather and tied together with a hard leather rope. They swing it over their heads and throw it at the cows' feet. Well, *womp, womp, womp*—God wrapped it around my ankles, and down I went. I was positively apprehended by that famous gaucho cowboy in the sky—JESUS! I was captured with his divine instrument. He knocks us off our feet, puts his foot on our necks, and then we say, "We found the Lord!"

The painting that triggered all this was by a famous Swedish artist named Birgitta Yavari-Ilan. I've had many supernatural experiences surrounding Birgitta's painting. God uses many ways to communicate with each of us, and in my case, he has repeatedly used this painting. He knows how to keep it interesting! We serve such a creative God. Don't all of you who have tasted of his love and mercy agree? If you will allow me to jump back and forth through time a bit, I would like to share a little more detail about this painting, which has been an anchor in my life.

In 1990, I was in Corona, California, discussing an upcoming missionary journey. I said, "Let's see, where does the Lord want to send us next? Let's choose from five countries. I see Brazil, Africa, Sweden, England, and Israel."

I paused to try to discern the mind of the Lord. Believe me, it's not always an easy matter to hear from God.

Then I said, "Let's choose Sweden."

Instantly the phone rang—*ring, ring, ring*. It was a Christian lady from an underground church in Bulgaria. She had escaped to Sweden and been living there for some years. Her voice sounded exactly like you'd expect a long-distance call from another country to sound.

She said, "The Lord showed me in a vision that I'm supposed to give you my flat in Stockholm, Sweden, this summer."

Can you believe it? Pretty big coincidence! I randomly said, "Let's pick Sweden," and seconds later we got a flat in Stockholm!

Two of us made the trip to Sweden. One evening after we were settled into this precious saint's flat in Stockholm, I shared with my Christian partner the story of my experience in Washington in 1978. I told him how, at the time, I could no longer endure "churchianity" and was planning to quit the ministry, but then the Lord used a religious painting of me in the bosom of Christ to change my mind. I explained that the Holy Spirit had come upon me and said I would never be able to leave the calling upon my life, so I've never tried to get out since then.

Literally fifteen minutes after I related that story, which, I remind you, had happened over a decade before, I went into the library in the flat where we were staying. It was lined with expensive and interesting books that I'm sure cost more than a hundred dollars each. They were beautiful. In Europe, people are very sophisticated in many ways. It seems to me that Europeans like to own good books and art and have an atmosphere of culture in their homes. It is very inspiring. We "middle-class colonials" should break out of our McDonalds and K-Mart mentality a little more than we do.

In this library there were books everywhere—huge stacks of books. I came up to a large bookshelf, also lined with literally hundreds of books, reached up to one particular stack, and then reached a little further to grasp a book that was entirely covered up by other books. It happened just like that. I didn't even know why I was choosing this particular one to look at, but the moment I touched the book, my hands began to burn like they were on fire. The heat in my hands felt like liquid electric energy. The very moment I grasped the book, the power of God hit my hands, and the Holy Spirit said, "Lonnie, guess what?"

It was the *exact* book that I had picked up on the coffee table in 1978. I said, "It must be the illustrated book with our picture in it."

And God spoke in his still, small voice and said, "You're right!"

"Wow, wow, wow!"

After I decided to stay in the ministry back in 1978 even though I was going through hellish trials, I went that very same year to spend some time in the Garden Tomb in Jerusalem. I needed a touch from God. I needed him to mend my heart. It was one of twelve ministry trips to Israel that I would go on. The Lord also had me live among the Palestinians as a mercy plea for those people. The Garden Tomb is another link to supernatural experiences for me, not to mention the site of the most glorious event in the history of the universe—the resurrection of Jesus Christ from the grave! That story can be found in the four Gospels.

However, on this particular trip back in 1978 at the Garden Tomb, to my complete surprise, there was Birgitta the artist sitting in the tomb, dressed in a World War II Red Cross nurse's uniform. She had moved from Sweden and started an orphanage.

I said to her, "Birgitta, remember me? You were my interpreter in Sweden in the revival that we had in 1971. You painted a picture of Jesus with me at a microphone in it."

She said, "Oh, Lonnie!"

Birgitta took me to her studio in Jerusalem and gave me a beautifully covered lithograph of the painting signed by the artist.

I want to close this account of the early years of my life and ministry, as I feel the touch of God surrounding Birgitta's painting. My heart's desire is that each person reading these words will have their own supernatural experiences with the Holy Spirit. He is our guide and only leads in one direction—to Jesus, the Savior and lover of our souls. Only he has the words of life. I know there are millions of you out there starving for the reality of God. So many who are sincere and hurt worse than I have been. This is your time. Today is the day of salvation.

Please pray with me: Yes, dear Lord, I am desperate to know what is really happening in this life. I am reaching out to you, Jesus, with the little measure of faith you have given each of us. Increase that faith and let it grow into a mighty tree planted in your kingdom. I receive you into my life. I give permission for your Spirit to come into my heart. Take me, God. Forgive all my sins, all my failures, all my past, and allow me to experience that new birth. Help me to follow wherever you lead, no matter what. I give you permission. I proclaim by simple faith that Jesus Christ came in the flesh and is the Son of the living God.

Let me be born again!

**"Not by might, nor by power,
but my spirit, saith the Lord!"**

Appendix

"Lonnie and Peter Pan"
by Stan Frisbee

As Lonnie's older brother by two years, I took on more of a protective role. Since we had an unstable home life and complicated childhood, we were close, but we were also very different. Lonnie had a Peter Pan syndrome: He didn't want to grow up, and he wanted to fly. He was always looking for something new to experience and loved turning people on to things. If he found something good, no matter what it was, he wanted people to have it too. So when he got older and experimented with drugs, he wanted others to feel the high.

Back in the fifties, most people were smokers and liked to drink. Most homes had built-in bars. You watch movies from that era, and the stars basically have a cigarette in one hand and a drink in the other. We called them juicers. But alcohol wasn't enough for us in the sixties. We were all about sex, drugs, and rock 'n' roll. Pot was a way to feel something, but in a different way. You didn't have a hangover. Like I said, Lonnie liked to turn people on, so he turned me, along with our friends and neighbors, on to pot as well. Everybody on our block started growing pot and selling it. It was cultural, a corporate thing, and music had a lot to do with it. Our whole society, at least everyone we knew, was getting loaded. We'd get dirt weed with all kinds of seed in it for ten dollars a bag. Later we got into speed, and then eventually Lonnie turned me on to LSD.

Lonnie also started experimenting with different forms of spirituality during this time, searching for love in all the wrong places. He had been interested in the New Age or even Pentecostalism as a boy and had a background of giving his life to the Lord when he was eight years old. Although he wasn't a walking, talking Christian as a teenager, he was still very curious about the more mystical side of life, always checking everything out for himself. He even tried to learn how to hypnotize people and things like that. He'd go up to Tahquitz Falls and take people with him—they called themselves "nudist, roper-doper hippies"—and they'd take off their clothes, drop LSD, and paint or just hang out. It was at Tahquitz Canyon where he later saw a vision from God and received the mantle to be an evangelist.

When he came back from the desert after that visitation from God, he would not stop talking about Jesus. We'd be at a friend's house, and someone would say, "If you don't shut up, you're going to have to leave," and he would talk, talk, talk, and then—"Out!" Lonnie lost his parents and all of his friends, even me. Then little by little, people started getting saved. Even though I didn't want to make a commitment to Christ, I knew it was real and from God. People would get saved and then **completely** change. There was no doubt about it. I also knew this wasn't just another phase for Lonnie. I watched him preach, and it was very dynamic, very real. I wasn't ready to be accountable to God yet (I liked my pot), but it was still special to watch my younger brother—who had been into all kinds of things—now baptizing people in the ocean. It was even more special to watch after I became a Christian during my time in the army. I'm sure Lonnie had me prayed in by old intercessor ladies. When I told him I was born again, he was absolutely elated. It was one of his dreams for me to get saved and become another comrade in the mission.

Some people have said, "Lonnie didn't have very much, but what he had he did a lot with." Well, I don't agree. Lonnie had a mantle from God, and that was a lot! That mantle gave Lonnie authority, and with that authority and his obedience, Lonnie did great things and saw miracles. My brother said he was a modern mystic. He was certainly an evangelist, catalyst, and forerunner. It wasn't something he decided to be—it was deep within him. The Holy Spirit worked through Lonnie, and even if it was a simple thing, it was a God thing. I believe the Lord chose my brother because, for one, God uses the weak, broken, and foolish things of the world to confound the wise and so-called mighty. But I also think it was Lonnie's childlike faith, open and vulnerable lifestyle, and his trust in God that qualified him—that made him willing to say **yes** to the incredible call on his life.

"The Jesus Movement Goes Mainstream"
by Jack Cheetham

Approaching 1970, the whole world seemed to be slowly coming apart in many different ways. The modern times, with the Vietnam War, numerous protests, and radical movements, were a bit too much for some people to bear, especially for kids who had never gone through major social change before. The idea struck me that people would most likely turn to religion during these uncertain times. I didn't cancel out any religion specifically, but I did believe that the Christian church would be the first religion to see that kind of significant ingathering. I had no inside knowledge or idea of this, as I was not connected to any church. I was a Methodist and my wife Betty an Episcopalian, but we were not necessarily "church people." We believed the basic Christian doctrine, yet had no serious involvement in religion at all. We were photographers, very new and not terribly sophisticated, but we had covered stories for different magazines before and were excited to find the story of some sort of Christian movement before it became mainstream.

We took our portfolio to New York, and I found an agent who agreed to take us on. I said to him, "There might be a big revival going on—a Jesus movement, and I'm going to go look for it. I think they're selling Jesus in the streets; I think they're selling Jesus in the alleys," which wasn't a put down, but simply just the slang of the day.

Our agent, of course, asked, "How do you know this?"

"I don't know," I told him, "I just think this is what's happening or what's about to happen."

Fortunately, the agent needed people in the field, so he didn't throw us out of the office, but many others probably would have. I was later archived in *Life* and then also in *Magnum*, and editors at those magazines would have shown us the door if we had brought that idea to them at the time. And so Betty and I drove to California in a truck with a good-sized camper and towed our little car behind it. The camper had a bathroom with a shower, a decent kitchen with a stove, and lots of other amenities. This was the only way we could afford to travel and search for the story.

We started looking and ended up in Ventura, California. One day we were at Oxnard, a town practically next door, doing laundry and reading the paper, and there was a story about a group of young people from Melodyland who were going to a nearby city to talk about the cultural drug problem and about how they were able to get off drugs. Well, to us Melodyland was associated with a group that originally put on New York City Broadway musicals, so we thought it must be a showbiz thing. We called our agent, and he said, "Yeah, go ahead, but don't waste too much film on it."

When we got to this meeting, all these young "showbiz" kids were talking about being saved by Jesus and how he got rid of their drugs. Each one had a very different testimony and came from a different walk of life. They were all nicely dressed, not like hippies of the time. Betty and I were fascinated, taking pictures like crazy all over the room. We actually bumped into each other back-to-back, and Betty turned her head and said over her shoulder, "I think you found the Jesus movement."

After the presentation was over, we talked with these kids about a movement of that kind, and they confirmed it. They said, "Oh yes, it's happening. There's Melodyland, Calvary Chapel, and Teen Challenge," and then they mentioned a number of other places. So we started checking them out, and we learned that my hunch was true: We had found the Jesus People movement, and there were *thousands* of people involved. All of this was still under the radar and had not yet reached national publicity.

So we began our nonstop whirlwind tour at Melodyland, a huge ministry led by a very kind minister, Ralph Wilkerson. Then we spent time with Teen Challenge members who were going all over the place to witness on the streets and present the gospel at schools. They provided us with the use of their darkroom to develop black-and-white film, and we sent the cans of color photos to New York.

We also covered a Pentecostal church, Bethel Tabernacle, whose members claimed they could get people off heroin in thirty seconds with no withdrawals. We definitely wanted to check this place out, and when we arrived, it was quite a wild scene. In one corner someone was playing a piano while people sang songs, and diagonally in the other corner, a fellow with drums and another with a trumpet were playing for their own little audience. People were jumping up and down, screaming, "Praise the Lord! Praise the Lord!" There were junkies there too who had track marks up and down their arms. People were laying hands on them and shouting Bible verses, and this went on for some time. Then suddenly the addicts would just come alive. Their eyes would open, and they were cured. I don't know how. I don't think I could ever explain it. Betty and I weren't shrinks or anything, but we thought that maybe when these heroin addicts had their emotions raised to such a high degree through the songs, prayers, and the overall atmosphere of the place, that somehow there was a transference in the brain. We saw those same people the next night, and they still had the tracks and everything, but they were no longer junkies.

Then we went to Calvary Chapel, which was quite large by then but still meeting at its smaller original building. This was where we met Lonnie Frisbee. Lonnie was a beautiful young man and had this aura, this glow about him. He had been delivered from the drug scene himself through Jesus, so he had a great deal to do with the religion and was always preaching everywhere he went. My wife and I thought it was fantastic how nothing ever seemed to faze him.

I remember Chuck Smith always announced every Sunday afternoon that they were going to go out to the Pacific Ocean to wash away sins and what have you and to baptize people. It was during this time when Betty and I had our born-again experiences.

This happened after sort of a culmination of everything we were seeing and hearing with the testimonies of the young people, and Lonnie played a big part in it as well. My wife and I were very aware of the drugs-and-rock 'n' roll era and could, shall we say, speak the language of the time. But after documenting part of the Jesus movement, we were greatly affected by it and even got baptized in the Pacific Ocean at Corona del Mar with the large crowds. I won't say that the color of the water turned black exactly, but that might give some idea about where I was coming from.

All of this happened so fast, and we were running like crazy to keep up. It was almost storybook how everything kept falling together for us, one page after another presenting itself, and just happening, happening, happening. Our agent took our pictures of the mass baptisms and packed-out church services to *Look*, and the managing editor told him, "I'm getting a feeling of mass here, not just one individual entity or organization or church, but a feeling of mass."

We didn't write this story. At the time, a major magazine story such as the one we were proposing would easily need twenty-five people on it to check everything, but there were just the two of us, and we were busy interviewing people like crazy. We had captions with all of the sheets explaining whom the people were in our interviews and photographs, where they were, what was going on. I am dyslexic, and back then we didn't have spell check, so Betty would have ended up doing most of the article writing. Even for Betty, an English major, the work was still a little too much and was moving too quickly, so the agent flew out a writer. He was there for just two days and then went back with all of my tapes and did the copy from there.

After *Look* picked up the story with their article "Today's Kids: Turning to Jesus, Turning from Drugs" in the February 9, 1971 issue, *Time* magazine also came aboard, and then *The Saturday Review* published "Children of Yearning: Meditations on the Jesus Freaks" on May 6, 1972. We also got coverage from many foreign magazines, such as *Bunte Illustrierte* in Germany, which used the headline, "Jesus ist besser als Hasch" ["Jesus is better than hash"], along with other magazines in Holland, France, and Spain.

Explo '72 at the Cottonbowl

Life magazine also took interest in this new movement, publishing "The Great Jesus Rally in Dallas" on June 30, 1972, and using our pictures for the cover and two-page inside spread of this candlelit service at the Cottonbowl. *Life* sent their own photographer, and he climbed up a tower at the infield to get the big record shot of the 130,000-person crowd. I stayed on the ground since I didn't want to take the time to climb up and risk missing something important. Sure enough, the wind blew all the candles out on one side, so the *Life* photographer didn't get any good shots from the above angle, while I got the side that still had candles lit. Someone with a little Instamatic camera took a picture, and then I used a cross-star filter to take one of a huge white cross off to the right side, so it was a winner.

Anyway, that's how Betty and I stumbled on to the Jesus People Revival. We went looking for a movement, and Jesus presented it to us very quickly. It was quite a time.

Photo by Jack Cheetham

193

Postscript
by Roger Sachs

I hope and pray that Lonnie's story, which is really God's story in our midst, has blessed you. Kathryn Kuhlman used to say, "God doesn't want golden vessels or silver vessels. He wants *yielded* vessels!" When I was working with Lonnie doing missionary trips, meetings, and working on his life story, I was constantly amazed by the presence of God surrounding him. If people could only experience God's presence—it changes lives. I knew it was God and not human charisma or personality although Lonnie had plenty of both. For all his strengths and weaknesses, he truly was a yielded, totally sold-out child of God.

Sometimes we would be driving on the freeways in Southern California, just the two of us, and he would start talking about something, and a normal moment would suddenly change. The presence of God would fill my little Ford Ranger, and the anointing on Lonnie's words would blow my mind. I would almost feel guilty. I'd think to myself, "He should be saying this to ten thousand people out there!" All of Lonnie's close friends will tell you the same thing: You never knew when a normal moment would turn into a divine encounter. You only knew that it happened all the time when Lonnie was around.

It is very exciting to finally get even a portion of Lonnie's story out there to the highways and byways. Lord willing, it will not take another twenty years to share the rest of his radical ongoing story. Lonnie's life actually accelerated after his part in the Jesus People movement. Some very, very good seasons lie ahead—and some very low points. We have the next powerful season of Lonnie's life ready to share, subtitled *The Great Commission*.

I am equally excited about all the audio and video that we have. We are, in addition, putting together an audio book, website, and a documentary featuring Lonnie himself. It is a huge task going through all of the material we compiled, but what a blessing! Pray for us because, as Lonnie often said, it's like the devil himself has put everything concerning Lonnie Frisbee on a hit list! There has been much resistance to getting the true story from Lonnie's personal perspective out there. I can attest to that.

Nevertheless, I would rather focus on the wonderful promise in Romans that says:

> If God is for us, who can be against us?...No, in all these things we are more than conquerors through him who loved us. For I am convinced, that neither death nor life, neither angels nor demons, neither the present nor the future, nor any powers, neither height nor depth, nor anything else in all creation, will be able to separate us from the love of God that is in Christ Jesus our Lord![77]

There are truths and tools that we can humbly embrace to become more than conquerors. The bottom line is that God wants to have a loving relationship with each one of us. It's the heart of the gospel, pure and simple. His presence is available to all who sincerely seek him.

Toward the end of his life, Lonnie wanted to give everything away. Anything good that God put on him, he wanted to give away and did with all of his heart. Lonnie followed the leading of our God, the all-time, ultimate giver!

God the Father gave us his Son.
Jesus gave us his life
—and sent us the Holy Spirit!

God bless you!
Roger Sachs

Endnotes

[1] Scriptural references for the Four Spiritual Laws: (1) John 3:16; 10:10; (2) Romans 3:23; 6:23; (3) Romans 5:8; 1 Corinthians 15:3–6; John 14:6; (4) John 1:12; 3:1–8; Ephesians 2:8–9; Revelation 3:20. For more information, check out Bill Bright's *Have you heard of the Four Spiritual Laws? 25 Tracts* (Campus Crusade for Christ, Inc., © 1965).

[2] Philippians 2:14–16

[3] TLB

[4] Leviticus 21:19

[5] Isaiah 55:11

[6] John 14:6; 10:7–11

[7] John 8:32 CEV

[8] Acts 2:44–45 NKJV

[9] 1 Corinthians 7:20

[10] 1 John 4:20

[11] Acts 2:17–18 NIV

[12] Numbers 6

[13] Jim Croce, "Time in a Bottle," *You Don't Mess Around with Jim.* ABC, 1972.

[14] Zechariah 4:6

[15] Acts 1:8

[16] Acts 2:17 NIV

[17] John 10:10

[18] Smith, Chuck and Hugh Steven. *The Reproducers: New Life for Thousands* (Philadelphia: Calvary Chapel of Philadelphia, 2011).

[19] John 21:25

[20] Psalm 75:6–7

[21] John 14:6 NKJV; See John 10:11

[22] Romans 6:1–2

[23] Psalm 30

[24] Mark 16:16; Acts 1:8

[25] Joel 2:28

[26] Acts 2:40; 1 Peter 4:5

[27] 2 Corinthians 5:17

[28] Ezekiel 36:26; John 4:14

[29] Matthew 10:32–33

[30] Deuteronomy 32:30

[31] Luke 10:20

[32] Acts 16:16–18 NKJV

[33] Luke 10:19; 20:43

[34] Mark 16:17

[35] Deuteronomy 32:30

[36] Matthew 12:43–45 NKJV

[37] Matthew 4:19

[38] Romans 8:14

[39] Matthew 25:21

[40] John 15:4–5 NIV

[41] Zechariah 4:6

[42] For more information about the founding of Vineyard Christian Fellowship in Kenn Gulliksen's own words, read *Not by Might, Nor by Power: The Great Commission*, Book Two.

[43] Proverbs 8:17

[44] Exodus 16

[45] Mike MacIntosh, *For the Love of Mike: The Mike MacIntosh story* (Thomas Nelson Publishers, 1984), 80-81.

[46] Psalm 103:12 NKJV

[47] Romans 8:28

[48] 2 Timothy 2:15 KJ21

[49] Matthew 8:14–15

[50] Luke 24:5–6

[51] Acts 10:44–46

[52] Numbers 14:18

[53] Mark 16:17

[54] Willie Nelson, "Little Old Fashioned Karma," *Tougher Than Leather*, Columbia, 1983.

[55] 1 Corinthians 15:55

[56] John 4:35

[57] Philippians 2:10

[58] Matthew 28:19–20

[59] Billy Joel, "Goodnight Saigon," *The Nylon Curtain*, Family Productions/Columbia, 1982.

[60] John 8:36 ISV

[61] Mark 16:17

[62] Luke 10:20

[63] Ephesians 6

[64] Daniel 3:25

[65] Daniel 3:18

66 Daniel 5:25

67 Isaiah 40:31

68 Psalm 3:6

69 2 Kings 6:17

70 Hebrews 12:2

71 John 16:33

72 Genesis 3:8

73 Luke 23:34

74 Psalm 139:8

75 Romans 8:28

76 1 John 3:20

77 Romans 8:31, 37–39 NIV

About the Authors

Lonnie Ray Frisbee (1949-1993) was an evangelist, missionary, and artist known to many as the "hippy preacher" who helped launch the Jesus People movement in the early 1970s. Raised in Southern California, Lonnie played a major role in the expansion of Calvary Chapel with Chuck Smith and Vineyard churches with John Wimber. Lonnie Frisbee influenced ministers and ministries around the world.

Roger Sachs is the founder and president of Freedom Crusade, the final ministry Lonnie was involved with before his death in 1993. He is the ghostwriter of Lonnie's authorized autobiography, *Not by Might, Nor by Power*, and has written his own life story, *Fire on the Mountain*. Roger currently lives with his wife, Roxanne, in Santa Maria, California.

Printed in Poland
by Amazon Fulfillment
Poland Sp. z o.o., Wrocław